About This Book

Have you ever felt that there had to be more to life than this? Have you ever fantasized that you have lived in other times and places? Have you ever met someone and felt an immediate kinship? Have you ever visited a strange place and felt that you had been there before? Have you struggled with frustrations and fears which seem to have no basis in your present life? Are you afraid of death? Have you ever been curious about reincarnation or maybe just interested enough to be skeptical?

Perhaps you believe in reincarnation and believe that you have lived before but haven't known how to tap your far memories. Maybe you have relied on someone else to tell you about lifetimes *they* think you lived. Or perhaps you found a 'how-to' book or tape but got discouraged because it took weeks, months or even years of following some mental regimen with no guarantee of results.

The **Practical Guide to Past Life Regression** presents a simple technique which you can use to obtain past life information TODAY. There are no mysterious preparations, no groups to join, no philosophy to which you must adhere. You don't even have to believe in reincarnation. The tools are provided for you to make your own investigations, find your own answers and make your own judgements as to the validity of the information and its usefulness to you.

This venture into your subconscious will provide high adventure and unusual insight into your self. Sample regressions and case histories are provided as examples of how others have used the information obtained with the technique to solve problems, strengthen relationships, overcome fears, be better parents, enhance talents, gain self-confidence, free themselves from detrimental habits and live a more positive, productive life.

The only things you need to unlock these experiences for yourself is this book, an hour of your time, and a friend who can read.

About the Author

Florence Wagner McClain is a parapsychologist, amateur archeologist, photographer, historian, expert woodsman and would-be pilot. She and her husband are in the process of building their own plane as an aid to their research. She has traveled and lived all over the United States.

She has spent almost thirty years in the study of the mind and experimenting with man's mental potentials, hypnosis, memory enhancement, the various psychic sciences (astrology, Tarot, numerology, scrying, clairvoyance, etc.) and metaphysics. She has spent more than ten years teaching and lecturing in the fields of mental and psychic development, and the practical applications in the field of education and in daily life. She has participated in approximately 2,000 past-life regressions, which is comparable to or in excess of the experiences of anyone working in that field.

To Write to the Author

We cannot guarantee that every letter to the author can be answered, but all will be forwarded on to her. Both the author and the publisher appreciate hearing from readers and learning of your enjoyment and benefit from this book. Llewellyn also publishes the *New Times*, a bi-monthly news magazine and catalogue of New Age studies and developments, and some readers' questions and comments may be answered through the *New Times'* columns if permission to do so is included in your letter. The author does participate in seminars and workshops, and dates and places may be announced in *The Llewellyn New Times*. To write to the author, or to secure a free copy of the *New Times*, write to:

Florence Wagner McClain
c/o THE LLEWELLYN NEW TIMES
P.O. Box 64383-Dept 510, St. Paul, MN 55164-0383, U.S.A.
Please enclose a self-addressed, stamped envelope for reply, or $1.00
to cover expenses.

Introduction

Past life regression, wisely used, is a valuable tool for enhancing the quality of your present life. King or serf, queen or kitchen maid — who or what you were in a past life is not nearly as important as who and what you are today. Social strata gained in past lives is important only to the immature ego. You are the sum of *all* of your past experiences. The important considerations are: What positive attitudes and strengths did you gain in past lifetimes? Are you making full use of them today? What mistakes did you make? Are you repeating the same self-defeating patterns in this lifetime? The more knowledge and understanding you have of your past experiences and how they affect your reactions to people, places and events, the nearer you are to true freedom and the age-old directive of "Know thyself".

How can we be certain that we have lived in other physical bodies in other times and places? Perhaps the only real proof, if one desires proof, lies in the individual personal experience of remembering past lives. But belief in reincarnation is not necessary to experience the benefits of past life regression. Re-living what seem to be past-life experiences can bring greater insight into yourself, clearer understanding of your strengths and weaknesses, and aid in clarifying your goals. Frequently answers to personal problems and problem relationships surface. Often it is possible to understand and gain freedom from phobias and detrimental habits. Prejudice and bigotry are difficult to maintain when you have remembered living in bodies of other races and passionately defending their beliefs. The concepts of 'male' and 'female' take on new dimensions. Remembering lifetimes as each sex, you come to understand that you are simply a soul which happens to inhabit a male or female body for this particular time. Death takes its place as just another phase in the natural cycle, instead of an end to be dreaded.

This method of past life regression is not presented as a magic cure-all. It is a tool to help you reshape your present self. The greater the care and precision with which you use it, the finer your finished product. Before you is a great adventure filled with laughter and tears, courage and cowardice, love and hate, compassion and cruelty, generosity and selfishness, and life and death. And, with it comes the understanding that in moments of great crisis we can all be heroes, but the real courage and challenge is in facing the routines of daily life with the best that is in within us.

What we did yesterday shaped today. What we do today shapes tomorrow.

A PRACTICAL GUIDE TO

PAST LIFE REGRESSION

Florence Wagner McClain

1986
Llewellyn Publications
St. Paul, Minnesota, 551164-0383, U.S.A.

International Standard Book Number: 0-87542-510-0
Library of Congress Catalog Number: 84-45285

First Edition, 1986
First Printing, 1986
Second Printing, 1986
Third Printing, 1986

Library of Congress Cataloging-in-Publication Data
McClain, Florence Wagner, 1938-
    Practical guide to past life regression.

    (Llewellyn's new age series)
    1. Reincarnation. I. Title. II. Title: Past life regression. III. Series.
BL515-M35 1985   133.9′01′3   84-45285
ISBN 0-87542-520-0

Cover Painting: Gloria McClain

Produced by Llewellyn Publications
Typography and Art property of Chester-Kent, Inc.

Published by
LLEWELLYN PUBLICATIONS
A Division of Chester-Kent, Inc.
P.O. Box 64383
St. Paul, MN 55164-0383, U.S.A.

Printed in the United States of America

TABLE OF CONTENTS

Chapter One

Definitions and Philosophy

"Such garbage I vud not feed you ven you vas Kind (child)," she said, eyeing the french fries. "Gut boiled potatoes I feed you. Come, I teach you to cook gut deutsch food." I stood in shocked silence as she continued. "Mommy, why are you the mother this time and I am the child? I don't want to be a child again."

A strange conversation made stranger still by the fact that the words came from the mouth of my tiny daughter a few months before her third birthday. Her first words had been in German. No one in our family or circle of friends spoke German. The phenomenon had lasted only a few weeks and I had been able to push it from my mind until now.

The following day she observed her older sister doing something of which she disapproved and turned to me. "I vud not allow you to behave so ven you vas Kind. You are not strict mit her. I do not vant to be a child again."

And so, I was forced to examine this strange belief

called reincarnation.

Reincarnation, regression, karma and other related terms mean different things to different people. For that reason it is important that I define these terms as I use them in this book and discuss some of the philosophy involved. The information presented here is the culmination of almost twenty years of personal investigation done through the means of some 2,000 past-life regressions. The definitions and principles presented are derived from those regressions and every effort has been made to present them in their simplest form. The information is presented for your consideration. The regression technique is presented as a means for your immediate investigation so that you may draw your own conclusions.

It is a tendency of man to claim for his own what he has discovered (however many millions may have made the discovery before him) and teach the method whereby he has made this discovery as 'The Only Way'. It is not my intention to convey that impression. This is one way among many.

What is Reincarnation?
Reincarnation is the theory that man's awareness, or soul, survives death and returns to be born again into a new physical body with renewed opportunity to progress and grow in knowledge and wisdom. It is a part of this belief that we experience life as both male and female, as members of all the various races and social classes, and that our many lifetimes encompass the whole gamut of good and evil. We have fought to free men from slavery and have bought and sold men as slaves. We have lived lives of celibacy and have sold ourselves for power and money. We have occupied places of authority and places of the most menial servitude.

The individual deeds are not as important as the motivations behind the deeds and whether we learned and grew from the experiences. We are the sum of our past experiences. We each have positive traits and talents as well as detrimental habit patterns and attitudes which have been developed in past lifetimes.

Many who do not fully understand the theory of reincarnation assume that those who do believe are attracted to the idea because, "You can just do whatever you want to in this lifetime and not worry about it because you have another chance". If anything, an investigation of reincarnation by means of past-life regression makes you more acutely aware of the consequences of each thought and action and the motivations behind them. The discovery that your past actions have created the difficult situations and undesirable personality traits you are dealing with now, as well as the goodness and beauty in your selves and lives, is a much stronger, more tangible motivation to use the best within us to create the best of futures than the threat of burning forever in some unimaginable hell.

At first, the idea of returning to live again and again seems comforting and inviting, especially to those who have a great fear of death. As knowledge and understanding increase, that aspect seems less inviting and the determination grows to learn and progress as quickly as possible so that the cycle of death and rebirth can be broken. "Mommy, I don't want to be a child again."

The purpose of reincarnation is for you to understand and claim your birthright as an evolving unlimited spirit created by and in the image of the ultimate Unlimited Spirit. When you understand your true nature and free yourself from limitations and accept full responsibility for your actions, then you have no further need to experience the lessons learned through physical existence on this earthly plane.

Reincarnation is one of the oldest and most widely held beliefs in the world. At the beginning of man's sojourn on earth his life was simple and closely integrated into the cycles of life, death, and rebirth which he saw all around him in nature. It was natural for him to believe that he, too, was a part of that cycle and his life would be renewed. And it is in those cultures across the world which continue to live in close harmony with nature where the most wide-spread belief in reincarnation has survived.

As man allowed his life to become more complicated and began to use the possession of material things as a measure of his self-worth, some made up rules to try and control others and benefit from their labors without personal effort. For some it was easy to allow others to take the reponsibility of telling them what to do, what to think and how to live their lives. It gave them someone to blame if things went awry. So man began to relinquish the freedom of being personally responsible for himself, his actions, and even his relationship with his Maker. And man forgot that he already knew the answer to the question which Job asked some 3,500 years ago, "If a man dies, will he live again?"

The techniques in this book are tools for you to use to help you remember what you already know and to rediscover yourself and provide your own answer to Job's question.

If you find that you come to a belief in reincarnation, you will be in good company. Consider these examples.

Shortly before the thirteenth Dalai Lama died in 1933, he related to trusted emissaries some of the circumstances which would surround his rebirth. In 1935, the acting regent had a vision which he wrote down and kept secret in which he saw the house and some of the surrounding buildings where a child had been born who was the reincarnation of the Dalai Lama. When the proper time came, the regent set out with search parties to find such a place and examine any children of the proper age. This was done quietly and discreetly, particularly since the search led them into a village across the Chinese border. A house was found which fit the description in the vision. The lamas exchanged clothing with their servants and allowed the servants to be greeted and entertained as dignitaries while they went to the kitchen area where the children were most likely to be found. There a boy of four years approached the head lama and correctly identified him as a lama from Sera. The child asked for the necklace the man wore, saying that it had belonged to him (the child) in his past life as the Dalai Lama. The child correctly identified the members of the party and later correctly identified many personal items which had belonged to the Dalai Lama from among many similar items. He met in every way the specifications which he had foretold about his own rebirth. Later the child successfully passed many stringent spiritual and physical tests which confirmed him as the fourteenth incarnation of the Dalai Lama.

While the great spiritual centers of Tibet were still in existence, before the Chinese occupation, it was not unusual for a young boy who showed exceptional knowledge and evolvement for his age, who was suspected to have been some great teacher or leader in a past-life, to be taken into a locked room where personal possessions of these great men were stored among thousands of other items. The boy would be asked to pick out those items which had belonged to him in a past life. If he successfully chose all the items which had belonged to one man, he was designated as a Recognized Incarnation and accorded the respect and honor due whatever position he had attained in the past.

One might say that John the Baptist was a Recognized Incarnation in a little different way. The prophecies in the Old Testament concerning the coming of the Messiah stated that Elijah, the prophet, would return first. (Malachi 4:5) In the book of Matthew (ch. 16: 13-14), when Jesus asked his disciples who people thought he was, they answered that some thought he was John the Baptist, some thought he was Elijah or Jeremiah or one of the other prophets returned. Later, after Jesus had acknowledged that He was the Christ, the disciples asked Him about the prophecy concerning Elijah's return to prepare the way. Jesus answered them that Elijah had already come again but that they hadn't recognized him. Then they understood that He spoke of John the Baptist. (Matthew 17: 10-13)

Then, there is the story in John 9: 1-3, of the man who had been born blind. The disciples questioned Jesus as to whether the blind man had sinned in some way which had caused him to be born blind, or if it was due to some sin of his parents. Without a belief in reincarnation and karma, the question is ridiculous and pointless. Jesus answered that in this instance neither situation applied, the man had been born blind that the glory of God might be manifested through him.

Do We Transmigrate?

Often the theory of reincarnation is confused with the theory of transmigration of the soul. "Oh, you believe that you come back as a cow or cockroach or something like that." Among those who believe in reincarnation, there is a relatively small group, mainly in India, which believes in transmigration of the soul. There is, however, no supportive evidence that man is ever reborn as anything but man.

It is probable that the theory of transmigration evolved from an ancient allegory which was meant to teach man's responsibility toward all forms of life. The spark of life which animates the cells of our bodies comes from the same Source which gives the spark of life to all living things. Therefore, there is a kinship between all life forms and that kinship should be recognized and valued and treated in a responsible manner.

Our physical bodies are made up of colonies of living cells, each performing a specific function to provide an efficient host for our souls. We are spirits who must function in a physical world. To be able to function, we must have a physical vehicle through which to manifest ourselves. Thus, we should value and show respect for and take reasonable care of the life forms which make up our bodies.

We are meant to be caretakers of the earth. We are responsible for the resources and all the life forms on this planet. We have the duty of establishing intelligent priorities for the use and treatment of life forms and resources. In many ways we have allowed our responsibilities to go unacknowledged and our priorities to become confused.

There were many groups among the American Indians who were true caretakers of the earth. (Though I put this in past tense, there are still many who practice these philosophies to the best of their abilities.) They revered this planet as a living entity and used the resources with care. They had no concept of personal ownership of the land. Mother Earth belonged to herself and to the Great Spirit who had created her. It was understood that the bounty of earth was here for man's use, but to be used thoughtfully, reverently, and with care that the resources were not wasted or depleted. If necessity demanded that they dig in the ground, this was treated as a wound on a living being. The soil was replaced and the wound 'healed' to the best of their ability. When it was necessary to hunt for food, Brother Deer or Elk or Bear was thanked and blessed for giving food, tools, and clothing. Every part of his body was put to use. Nothing was killed for sport. There was a definite purpose or need behind every action.

Today, in our throw-away society, we thoughtlessly use and waste the resources of Mother Earth and do little or nothing to replace them and heal her wounds. We have allowed ourselves to devalue ourselves by using what and how much we own as a measure of self-worth. As long as we can spend thousands of dollars to spoil and pamper a pet while the child down the block goes to bed hungry, and then abandon the pet or its offspring when we tire of them to starve or be maimed or killed along the highways, then our priorities will remain confused, we will feel alone and alienated from our Source of Life, and our steward-ship of earth will be a failure.

Are You an Old Soul?

It is not uncommon for those pursuing an interest in reincarnation or other metaphysical subjects to be told at one time or another, "You are an old soul". Most people have no real idea of what that means except that it sounds mysterious and makes them feel special. Being an old soul would seem to imply that the soul had been around longer than most and, therefore, possessed some secret knowledge or wisdom which sets it apart from others.

Actually, we are all old souls, chronologically speak-ing. Regression evidence (our own as well as that of other researchers) indicates that all souls were created at the same time — a very long time ago. Some souls have lived more lifetimes than others. They might be said to be older in experience. Like students in school, it takes some of us longer to learn than others. Some understand and pass a subject the first time. Others must repeat a subject one or more times to understand. The fact that we are still here, involved in the cycles of life, death and rebirth, indicates that we still have lessons to learn. So, being an old soul isn't a status symbol. It is just a fact of life.

Allowing yourself to be drawn into the 'old soul' rou-tine can cause serious problems. There are great pitfalls in attempting to judge the level of another's spiritual evolvement. You are the only human being who knows your every motivation and innermost thought. To judge another on the basis of career, appearance, social status, outward signs of spirituality, or even intuitive feelings, is to assume a role you have no right to and for which you lack the wisdom. Even more dangerous is to allow your evaluation of your own spiritual evolvement to rest on the words of someone else.

Even self-evaluation must be undertaken with care. Mankind often somehow finds it easier to acknowledge faults and weaknesses than talents and strengths. It is the mark of a mature soul to be able to matter-of-factly recognize and acknowledge positive character traits along with the not so positive. A balanced viewpoint in self-evaluation is to think in terms of *the tools you have to work with* and *the areas you need to work on*, rather than good and bad or positive and negative.

Do You Have a Soulmate?

Soulmate is a frequently misunderstood and misused term. Often it is used to put forth the idea that somewhere you have a twin soul, or the other half of you, which is your true mate and you are destined to be together. It sounds very romantic — the stuff of fairy tales. But there is no evidence to support the idea that, in all of the Universe, there is but one soul who is your true mate.

In actuality, you are far more fortunate than that. Through the eons of your existence, there have been many souls with whom you have experienced love, friendship, varieties of learning experiences and evolvement into similar levels of awareness through many lifetimes. There are strong, deep bonds with these soul friends or soul siblings which often transcend simple friendship or even romantic love. You have shared the joys, sorrows, triumphs, failures, tears and laughter of life together. You have seen each other at your best and at your worst. With each experience the bonds between you become stronger. Upon meeting for the first time in this lifetime, you may feel an immediate kinship and stirrings of deep emotions. You may feel little or no need to maintain the protective facades we often use with each other or play the social games which have become so much a part of daily life.

You and your soul friends often reincarnate in times and places so that your paths cross again and again, strengthening your bonds. Usually the reason for this is because you are working on similar areas of growth. In some instances it is possible that two or more of you have made a commitment to work together through several lifetimes to bring about certain spiritual, social or technological changes in the world.

The soul friend relationship, in some cases, may be a relatively new relationship. In each lifetime, in each relationship, we plant the seeds for the growth of new soul friends. As the patterns develop, you will notice that one of the most outstanding characteristics of the relationship is that you don't think of each other in terms of race, sex, age, appearance or any other outward trapping. You are one soul recognizing another, understanding that everything else is simply costuming for this present lifetime.

Having one or more soul friends in your life can be one of the most exciting, rewarding experiences imaginable. We are here to broaden our base of experience and learn to live in harmony with all mankind as far as possible. A soul friendship can be a most positive pattern and influence for this goal. A mature soul friendship does not exclude others. It draws others into the circle.

Whether you are concerned with building better relationships with people in general, or perhaps with your husband or wife in particular, an examination of your soul friend relationship is a prime place to start. What makes the relationship special? The respect and tolerance you show to each other? The courtesy and patience with which you really listen when the other talks? Allowing each other the right to hold differing opinions about things? The openness with which you are able to talk about your feelings, fears, hopes and goals? Feeling free to just be yourself? Allowing yourself and the other person the right to argue or even become angry, with the knowledge that it doesn't change the love between you? Being able to laugh at yourselves together? Being able to admit mistakes to each other?

Cultivating these attitudes and actions can cause your relationships with others to take on new life and dimension. If it is a marriage you are concentrating your efforts on, it can become the 'stuff of fairy tales' and more. If you become the type of person you would like your friends or mate to be, your life will be rich in all the things that really count — the things which last beyond a lifetime.

Past-Life Regression

Past-life regression is tuning into the subconscious to recall memories of past experiences. It can happen in many ways. Sometimes the experience happens spontaneously, prompted by a person, place or event which jogs the memory.

Many years ago, before I had experienced regression, I was drawn to the romantic anti-bellum South. I thought that if there was such a thing as reincarnation, which I strongly doubted, I must have lived a life as a dainty southern belle. I sometimes daydreamed about what such a life might have been like. Then, one summer, I visited the Civil War battle site at Vicksburg, Mississippi, and the southern belle image was shattered forever.

As we drove through the battleground, the car and its passengers were barely real to me. It took every shred of control I had to respond to the ongoing conversation. I vaguely remember one of the children saying, "I wish the battle was still going on so we could see it." For me, it was.

The air was filled with the smells of smoke, gunpowder, and blood, and the cries of wounded and dying. The sounds of battle were all around me. The Union Army was slaughtering us. I was following my men in retreat over an embankment, terrified that a bullet would find its mark in my back before I reached cover. I knew my name and where I had come from and how I came to be there. I was as aware of who and what that man was and all of his history as I am of my present self.

Later, as our party stood before the Confederate memorial which listed the names of those who had died there, there were certain names which brought tears to my eyes and vivid memories of the faces of friends and comrades who had fallen during those bloody summer days of 1863. The Civil War no longer had any romantic appeal for me.

I was shaken and frightened by the experience. The people I was with strongly disbelieved in anything of a psychic nature, so I could not discuss it with them. By the following day when I arrived home, I was practically a basket case. I collapsed in tears in my husband's arms and sobbed out a semi-coherent account of the experience. We were both baffled by the occurrence, but my husband assured me that he didn't think I was losing my sanity. During the following days we both tried to forget what had happened.

A few weeks later I was sitting in the waiting room of a doctor's office. The doctor was a Civil War buff and the bookcases in the waiting room were filled with volumes on the subject. I took one of the older volumes and began to turn through, idly looking at the photographs. I still remember the cold panic I felt when I saw 'my face', identified with 'my name' and a short biographical sketch verifying 'my memories'. I slammed the book closed and ran from the office.

Looking back, my reactions seem rather melodramatic.

But, I had no understanding, at that time, of what had happened to me. The incident went against everything I had been taught to believe. Only crazy people saw and heard things which weren't there, and thought they were someone else. None of my religious beliefs supported such a happening. Part of me was terrified that I was becoming mentally unstable. Another part of me was equally terrified at having to re-examine and question my lifelong religious beliefs. But, down deep in some inner core of myself, I KNEW that the experience had been real and that somehow I had lived a lifetime in which that Confederate soldier was me.

Spontaneous regressions are not always that vivid or detailed, but even less dramatic experiences can shake a person badly when there is no knowledge or understanding to go with them. I suspect that there are thousands of people who have had similar episodes and have repressed them out of fear and lack of understanding.

Meditation is another method by which past-life memories can be recalled. It is not unusual for those who practice meditation regularly to catch glimpses or impressions of past-life experiences. Quite often, concepts which have been previously understood and knowledge which has been learned in previous lifetimes are brought into the conscious mind in this way.

Small children often have clear memories of past-life experiences which fade as they get older. The daydreams they experience, the sequences they imagine or 'play-like' often have roots in those memories. All too often parents are too busy to listen, or discourage daydreaming and the exercise of the imagination as something undesirable. So, as children get older they tend to suppress these mental activities which are meant to be developed as tools for living a full life.

Twenty or thirty years ago, when a child's exposure

to the world was more limited, it was much simpler to separate legitimate past-life memories from childish fantasies prompted by stories to which the child had been exposed. With the advent of television and its too common use as a babysitter, it is often difficult or impossible to know for certain which is past-life memory and which is information derived from a television program.

Children's dreams, as well as those of adults, sometimes have bits and pieces of past-life memories. I suspect that nightmares and recurrent troubling dreams may often have their basis in some unhappy or frightening experience from the past.

I do not encourage actively attempting to elicit past-life memories from young children. Simply listen to what is volunteered and observe ways in which the information may help explain behavior patterns or insecurities. Peculiar behavior patterns may themselves be clues to past-life experiences.

Our oldest daughter, as soon as she was old enough to make her wishes known, began to refuse to leave the house for even the distance of a few blocks unless she had a container of water and a small packet of food. She seldom used either item while we were out. Initially, I attempted to put a stop to this, but her reaction was so out of character that I knew this was more than a childish whim. Gradually I was able to change this behavior by showing her that I had money with me, or giving her money, and assuring her that we would stop and buy something if she became hungry or thirsty.

When I considered this behavior in conjunction with the fact that, from time to time while cleaning her room, I would find a half of a sandwich or a piece of cheese, or an apple or carrot or some other bit of food neatly wrapped in a napkin and hidden, I realized that she had some deeply rooted insecurity involving food. There was no reason in this lifetime that I could determine. She was far too young to regress (3-4 yrs.), so I simply made certain that there was always fruit or some snack within her reach. Gradually she stopped hiding food.

In later years, we discovered that she had starved to death in what was probably her most recent lifetime. At age twenty, she admits that occasionally when she goes out without enough cash in her purse to buy a meal, she feels a tiny, momentary twinge of uneasiness, but understanding the cause, it is not a problem.

We could easily have caused deep trauma to this child if we had handled this situation as a behavior problem which called for discipline rather than understanding.

One of the greatest things that we can do for our children in relation to possible past-life influences is to listen to them and observe their behavior patterns with patience. Encourage positive patterns and provide opportunities for any positive talents to be developed. Observe negative or unusual behavior and attempt to determine if this is simply normal behavior for the particular age, or an overall personality trait, or if it is an isolated pattern outside the normal behavior of that child which is consistently triggered by the same type of situation. Sometimes simply asking the child why he or she reacts to a certain situation in a particular way will elicit valuable information. This should be done carefully at a time when the child is relaxed and happy. If a fear is expressed which has no basis within the present experience of the child, reassure him that while that thing which he fears may have happened at some time in the past, this is a different time, a different place, and different circumstances and he no longer needs to be afraid. Then make every *reasonable* effort to make the child feel secure in those particular areas.

No matter how bizarre or strange a fear or concern may be, don't laugh or belittle it. Little can be more frightening and upsetting to a child than to have a fear which is very real to him, but is not taken seriously by those on whom he depends for security and safety. And, he may have a very real basis for the fear.

The child who is afraid of the dark and wants a night-light may be the POW who was kept in a dark hole for weeks or months before he died. The child who has an inordinate fear of water may have drowned. How cruel to make an issue of such fears and ridicule them and force such a child to stay in the dark or go into the water. A child will overcome many fears on his own, given time, patience and positive support in a secure environment.

One of the most valuable things you can do for your child is to encourage a healthy imagination and allow him time for daydreams. These are creative tools which he will use throughout his lifetime. Nothing was ever created or accomplished which wasn't first created in the imagination, and active use of the imagination helps tap the resources of all your many lifetimes.

Déjà vu is a term often associated with reincarnation and past-life memory. It is a French term meaning seen before or already seen. It is usually applied to instances in which you have the sudden feeling that you have had the particular conversation you are having before, or have been in the place where you are with the same people before. Often this is due to having had a prophetic dream which you don't consciously remember, or a type of precognitive instant-replay.

Occasionally *deja vu* relates to a past-life experience. A year or two prior to my experience at the Civil War battle-field, I went on a camping trip into an area of the South-west where I had never been during this lifetime. The area was rough and wild, but uncannily familiar. I knew what would be around each bend in the canyon and I recognized certain unusual rock formations. I felt more at home there than any place I had ever been. Some years later, having experienced several regressions, I had occasion to return to the same area in the company of several friends who had also been regressed. The area was as familiar to them as it had been to me. We realized that over several centuries we had lived many lifetimes in that place.

We desired to test our memories and our regression experiences. From the past-life information we knew where certain special places should be — a hidden waterfall, a childhood hidey-hole, a lover's trysting place, a tomb, the ruins of a village, an ancient place of worship — and though they were in remote areas where ncne of us had been in this lifetime, we were able to go directly to them.

Conventional hypnosis is probably the most frequently used method for past-life regression. Done by a careful, competent hypnotist who has no prejudice against the theory of reincarnation, it is a very effective method. However, it can be difficult to find a competent professional hypnotist who believes in reincarnation and is experienced in conducting past-life regressions. It can also be an expensive project.

The main drawback in the use of conventional hypnosis is the lack of conscious involvement on the part of the person being regressed. It is possible for the hypnotist to overlook significant clues to areas which should be more fully explored. Sometimes, through carelessness or over-eagerness, questions are asked in such a way as to suggest answers to the subconscious. It is possible, also, for the hypnotist to force one's recall into areas of traumatic or embarrassing situations. Often, also, the person being regressed must rely heavily on the hypnotist's record of the regression rather than his own memory. Depending upon the method of record keeping used, the hypnotist's version of the regression information may be colored by his own interpretation.

Using the regression method presented here, you may choose the direction of the investigation of a past-life experience *during* the regression. You may terminate the session at any point which you choose and you have full recall of the events re-lived. You may make your own choice about re-living a potentially uncomfortable or traumatic experience. You have the control to avoid answering questions which you choose not to answer and yet retain the information for your own use. You can be guided through the regression experience by any reasonably responsible person of your choice, in your own home, at your convenience, without cost. And, after a few regressions, if you choose, you can regress yourself.

What is Karma?

Karma is the law of cause and effect. It is the meeting of self, the reaping of what has been sown. The purpose of karma is *not* to punish, but to teach and help us learn to live in harmony with the Universe.

The law of cause and effect is a Universal Law. For every action or cause there is a reaction or effect. That is unchanging and beyond our control. What is within our control is the action or cause we set into motion and the attitude with which we deal with the effect. It is our attitude which makes karma into a negative or positive influence in our lives. Karma, of itself, is neither good nor bad. Karma just is.

Karma is most often spoken of in terms of karmic debt, or in terms of suffering or the unpleasant aspects of our lives. Seldom do people think of or mention the riches of knowledge, wisdom, skills, talents, friends and loved ones which are the result of past-life actions, and thus, also a part of the law of cause and effect — our karmic heritage.

If you wear shoes which are too small, your feet will hurt. Cause and effect. You have two choices as to how to deal with the situation. You can continue to wear the shoes and be miserable and possibly cause serious damage to your feet, and probably become grumpy and make others around you miserable, or you can learn from the experience and wear shoes which are comfortable and be free to focus your mind on other things. This may seem like a simplistic explanation of karma, but this is essentially what karma is all about.

The common view of karma is that if you caused someone to suffer in a past life, then you must suffer in this one. To what end? How will generating more suffering in this world benefit you or anyone else? How much more positive and good to have those energies turned to the alleviation of suffering.

Part of our spiritual evolvement is coming to the understanding that karma is not meant to be a system of punishment and reward, but a learning experience whereby we gain wisdom. Then we can use that wisdom and our free will to choose the paths of learning which will be the most positive and beneficial to ourselves as well as others. An added benefit of understanding the instructive purposes of karma is that if you have come to an understanding of a concept or principle and have made it a part of your life, then it is not necessary to live out a sequence of events to satisfy the 'effect' aspect.

Our talents, skills, the instinct which successfully guides us through new or difficult situations, self-confidence in certain areas of our lives — these are all results of our past actions. We have, in our eons of living, gained an incredible amount of knowledge and expertise in a vast number of areas. Some fields of endeavor we have pursued to the fullest. Others we have abandoned for one reason or another. But that knowledge is still a part of us and, if we so choose, it can be retrieved for use in our present lives through the means of past-life regression.

As an example: Several years ago certain events awakened my interest in herbal and folk medicine. Though I wanted to know as much as possible on the subject, other demands on my time did not permit an intensive study of the subject. I was delighted to discover three lifetimes, in various parts of the world, in which I had been very knowledgeable on the subject. A couple of hours spent reviewing the experiences of those lifetimes greatly increased my present conscious knowledge of the subject, which when implemented with a small amount of reading (mostly to check out the validity of some of the 'remembered' information), I was able to put to use a short time later when some emergencies occurred and conventional medical help was unavailable.

This was karma at work. The initial actions were the lifetimes spent in study of the subject, the effects that the knowledge was there to be retrieved. Then, the action of retrieving the knowledge was followed by the effect of being able to successfully put the knowledge to use in some life threatening situations.

We deal with the law of cause and effect every hour of every day. Often we also have to deal with the effects of other people's actions — but even then we have a choice as to how we let it affect us. If you don't pay your electric bill, the electricity will be turned off. If you do pay your bill, it stays on — unless, perhaps someone crashes into a lightpole and breaks the line. That affects you. You can fume and fret and make irate calls to the utility company, and cuss or sulk and make it into a really miserable experience. Or, you can accept the situation and be creative and imaginative and turn it into an adventure which you and your family will remember as a very special time. It's your choice.

If I seem to belabor the subject of karma, it is because it is so important that you understand that karma is not some sword of Damocles hanging over your head, waiting to come crashing down and inflict some terrible wound in your life. Understanding karma can help you gain a perspective on what is really important in your day to day life and what isn't. Understanding is learning the necessary lesson of accepting personal responsibility for your life and the vital importance of attitude.

You do what you really want to do. That can be a difficult idea to accept, because accepting it means you accept personal responsibility for the circumstances of your life. Accepting it means that you can no longer blame circumstances or karma, or someone or something else for the state of your life.

You *think* that you are doing many things that you don't really want to do. You *think* that you are not doing other things that you would like to do. Let's examine the truth or fallacy of those statements.

Probably the most common complaint is that you don't like your job. Then why are you still working at it? Is it easier to stay and complain than to put out the effort to find another job? Or perhaps you are afraid to try something different? Better something familiar than to venture into the unknown? Perhaps jobs are difficult to find where you are and you feel lucky to have one even though you don't like it. Maybe the job you have is a necessary step on the way to where you want to be. Perhaps it is the only type of work you are trained to do. Have you made any effort to find a way to get other training?

You see, if you ask yourself the questions and have the courage to be truthful to yourself, you will see that you have stayed on that job or in that situation because *you* made the choice. Either you were not willing to pay the price necessary to make the change, or surrounding conditions made it more reasonable to stay in that situation at the present time.

The same type of questioning applies to the reasons you are not doing certain things you would like to do. The most common excuse people use is that, while they would like to do a certain thing, they don't believe they could. You never know until you try.

There have always been those who have risen above mental, physical, emotional, social and/or economic handicaps to succeed in reaching the goals they have set for themselves. They are people who refuse to quit. If one door closes in their faces, they try another and another. They refuse to accept defeat. They know that they are responsible for themselves and their successes or failures. Failures are used as learning experiences to generate successes.

There have always been those who have been content to blame circumstances or anyone or anything outside themselves for their situations. They spend their lives whining and bemoaning their 'fate', never making any effort to change anything. After all, if they tried, they might fail. If you never try anything, you never fail. Even worse, they might succeed and have to accept the fact that the situation was within their power to change all along.

More often than not, a change in attitude is the key which opens the door to success and happiness. Many years ago I had reached a very low point in my life. My existence seemed pointless, boring and filled with one irritation after another. One day I was griping at my oldest daughter, who was only 3, about her persistent explorations of a vacant lot filled with dead weeds taller than my head. She took me by the hand and led me into the tangle of brown stalks and pointed to a profusion of tiny, exquisite flowers which carpeted the ground. "Mommy, little girls don't see the weeds," she said, "they just see the flowers."

Her words kept running through my mind. I couldn't shut them out. The more I thought about them, the more uncomfortable I became because those words took on a deeper meaning. I finally admitted to myself that I awoke each day looking for and expecting nothing but weeds in my life. I had allowed myself to be blind to the flowers. I had two beautiful, healthy daughters, a loving husband and family, a lovely new home and many friends. I had a good mind which I wasn't using and talents which I ignored.

I made a consistent, conscious effort to greet each new day looking for and expecting flowers. The circumstances of my life didn't change, but my attitude did and my life became interesting and exciting. Suddenly doors began to open which led into some strange and wonderful pathways. Probably they had been there all the while, but I had been too busy cataloging the weeds to see them.

Your attitudes toward yourself and others will have a direct bearing on how valuable your past life regression experiences will be to you. Seeing the weeds will help you to understand what has grown in your garden of life in the past and what seeds may be buried in the ground waiting for rebirth. But the flowers which are alive and flourishing in your life are your most important considerations. Nourish them and encourage their growth by uprooting the weeds. Put the weeds in a mental compost pit so that they can decay and transform themselves into nourishment for the flowers. With a positive attitude and determination you can find something in almost any situation which can be shaped and used to your benefit.

Chapter Two

Setting the Scene

It is important to take care in setting the scene for your first regression experiences. Because it is a new experience and perhaps a little scary, it is important that you choose a place where you feel physically and mentally comfortable and aren't tense about possible interruptions. Later, when you are comfortable with the idea of regression and have gained some expertise, you will find that you can be regressed with the television going, the kids yelling, the telephone or doorbell ringing, or even regress yourself while you are doing the dishes or mowing the lawn. But that's for later.

Choose a quiet place where you are unlikely to have interruptions, where you can pull off your shoes and recline. It's usually a good idea to have a sheet or light cover handy because people often feel slightly cool during a regression. It is a good idea not to be too far away from a restroom. You will be working at the particular levels of mental activity where bodily processes are speeded up, and more often than not, you will probably experience an urgent need to empty your bladder by the end of the regression. This is perfectly normal.

For your first regression experience, you may be more comfortable working with just one other person. And then again, it may not matter to you. (One gentleman of my acquaintance was adamant that his wife not be present during his first regression. He was certain, mistakenly so, that he had been a coward in battle and was embarrassed for her to know.) Choose someone you are completely comfortable with to conduct your first regressions. If you are concerned about what others may think about you, you will be paying more attention to that than to the regression.

Regressions can be conducted with several people present with more than one person asking questions. But, past-life regressions are not party games and should not be done in a party atmosphere. You get out of a regression about what you put into it.

Mental and Emotional Attitudes

Persons being regressed are vulnerable to the emotional and mental attitudes of those around them. Every effort should be made to keep the atmosphere positive and light. A healthy sense of humor is not out of place and will often help ease tension. Avoid cultivating the feeling of the regression being a test. This is not a pass or fail situation. This is an experience in reacalling memories from the far past. Just as it is easier for some people to recall detailed memories from early childhood than it is for others, so some, at first, will find it easier to recall detailed memories from other lifetimes.

I remember regressing one dear little lady who could remember every tiny detail of an uneventful lifetime so boring that it almost put both of us to sleep. We knew what her family ate for every meal and just how the table was set, and every other mundane detail of everyday life, but learned nothing of any real significance to her present situation. The only reason we persisted with that regression was that we thought surely something had happened in that lifetime. But she died in the same house she was born in and one day varied little from the next. So, more is not necessarily better.

In another regression, a man regressing for the first time had only vague and fleeting impressions of several lifetimes. He remembered no names, no dates, and had only slight impressions as to settings and events. This proved to be a very significant experience for the man because there was a recurring pattern of being a 'loner' in each lifetime. He gained a great deal of insight into his present attitudes toward people and some of the reasons for some difficulties in his present lifestyle.

Records

Keeping records is an important part of past-life regressions. I have found written records to be the most valuable for me. It is easier to insert notes as additional details are remembered and easier for me to pick out important bits of information from written material than from listening to tapes. At first, written records are only really practical if there is a third person present to take notes. Trying to learn the technique for conducting a regression and attempting to take notes at the same time can get to be like trying to juggle raw eggs for the first time — nerve wracking.

If you are taking notes, often the answer will be enough to tell what the question was. If not, include a few key words so that later the reader will understand the question. If you don't understand what the person being regressed has said, feel free to ask him to repeat it.

Some people freeze up in the presence of a tape

recorder or, at the very least, become self-conscious. By all means, use a tape recorder if it doesn't disturb the regressee — but make certain that you are getting a good tape. Nothing is more frustrating than an interesting regression accompanied by a blank or inaudible tape. I would suggest that someone transcribe the tape into a written record, also.

Why keep records? Very often information which doesn't seem significant at the time can prove to be important at a later date. Perhaps later regressions, when studied with the earlier records, will point up trends or patterns that were not evident at first. Also, careful study of records often produces insight which may have been missed during previous study. I recently scanned some records of some of my own regressions done about ten years ago. I got some very important insight into some present situations in my life from some patterns which had no meaning for me when the regressions were done. I won't begrudge those records their space in my files any more.

Another reason to keep records is that after a regression you will find that you will remember a great deal more than you verbalized, and those additional details can add a great deal of meaning and insight into the regression.

General Instructions

For the person directing the regression: Keep a positive, relaxed attitude. Conducting regressions can be valuable experiences for you in your own regressions. Also, the more expertise you gain in conducting regressions, the better you will be at asking questions and eliciting important information. Above all, keep a positive, relaxed attitude. This is not a pass or fail situation for you either, and the world won't come to a screeching halt if you aren't letter perfect with the technique.

There are some points which are important for you to

keep in mind. You aren't obliged to regress every one who asks you. Avoid regressing anyone who is obviously deeply mentally or emotionally disturbed. Leave them to the professionals. Also, avoid providing a showcase for exhibitionists or attention seekers. Your time is too valuable to waste on people who are only interested in playing games.

Be observant during the regressions. Watch for signs of undue stress or tension. Those signs are: agitated hand movements or tightly clenched fists, a clenched jaw, abnormal or uncontrolled laughter, tears when combined with any of the other signs. Tears alone are not necessarily something to be concerned about as they are often a healthy catharsis, especially if they are appropriate to the particular incident. If you should be faced with a situation where the person being regressed is obviously in great distress, calmly and matter-of-factly ask if something is bothering them and if they would prefer to end the regression or skip that event and go on to something else. Calmly remind them that they are "here and now". Tell them, "This is simply an exercise in remembering. There is no need for you to experience any pain or distress of any kind on any level."

If the person being regressed indicates that he or she would prefer to end the regression, repeat the positive statements at the end of the regression technique. If he or she wants to continue, simply give instructions to progress to a time; a week, month, year, or whatever span of time seems appropriate after that incident, and proceed. After the regression it may be a good idea to discuss whatever was causing the distress if the person wants to. The memory will have been triggered and sometimes it is easier to discuss it and deal with it outside of a regression with less emotional involvement. Do not press the individual to talk about the incident if they show reluctance, but do provide a sympathetic, non-judgemental atmosphere in any case. Do let them know that discussing whatever caused the distress will help release the emotions involved and put it in perspective and make it easier to deal with. But don't insist.

Over a period of almost twenty years, involving over 2,000 regressions, I have never had a situation which developed into a traumatic experience when handled in this manner. Seldom, if ever, will you encounter any situation of undue distress in a regression experience. Forget the dramatic scenes you may have seen in movies and on television involving regressions. They have little, and in most instances nothing, to do with real life regressions. And you cannot regress a person into a past life situation and get them trapped so that he or she cannot return to the present time and place.

The regression technique is structured in such a way as to have some built-in safeguards and to avoid certain words or phrases which have been found to sometimes trigger negative responses in the general public. But the most important part of the regression technique is the emphasis on it being an exercise in remembering, and the positive closing statements.

While you are conducting a regression, accept whatever answers are given to your questions. Do not question or argue with the answers. This is not a part of your function. Also, be careful that you do not ask leading questions, even if you have impressions of what the person regressing is seeing or experiencing. If the person is not getting clear impressions about his or her surroundings, for instance, and you are, do not ask, "Are you in a house?" Instead ask, "Are you inside some structure or are you outdoors? Are you in the country, a town or village, or a large city?" Give them a choice and their minds will focus on the right answer.

Keep the person observing and conversing. Don't let them get bogged down in tedious detail. Don't spend too long at any one point in a lifetime. Keep them moving in time. Lifetimes can be explored in more detail after a couple of regression experiences have made the person feel at home with the technique. Often further detail explorations may prove unnecessary because of spontaneous memories triggered by the initial regression to a lifetime.

Frequently emphasize that, "This is simply an exercise in remembering."

The first regression experience should be limited to approximately an hour. Later regressions may be prolonged as is comfortable and appropriate. The passage of time is distorted at the particular levels of mind where you will be working. The regression period may seem much longer or shorter than it actually is.

Above all, remember that in conducting a regression your function is to assist in focusing attention by asking questions, not to assume control of the person or the session. Conducting a regression is easy. You deal with more difficult situations every day. It is normal, at first, to be a little tense in any new situation, but the more relaxed and at ease you can be, the more relaxed and at ease the person being regressed will be. People tend to fear the unknown and the mind is one of the great frontiers left for exploration. But keep in mind that we are minds, or spirits, or souls — however you may desire to think of it — and so that great frontier is US.

For the person being regressed: Relax. This is simply an exercise in exploring your memory. There are no right or wrong answers. Answer the questions asked with the first impressions which come to mind. Don't try to think out your answers or correlate impressions with generally accepted fact. Often information which is at variance with recorded history later proves to be accurate. In numerous instances recorded history has little or nothing to do with what actually happened.

You may receive information in any or all of several ways. Some individuals feel that they are actually participating in re-living a particular lifetime with all the accompanying sensory input. More commonly the sensation is one of being an observer and watching the events unfold. Others may have little or no visual impressions but may hear, taste, smell, feel and/or generally sense surroundings and events. There are some who get the main part of their information through physical sensations. Others seem to have no real sensory input but simply 'know' the answers to the questions.

No one way of receiving information is any better or more accurate than another. Of course, many of those who do not receive visual impressions tend to fret about it and sometimes allow that to get in the way of the information they are receiving. I have a dear friend who is one of the finest psychics I have ever known. His information is detailed and accurate. He does not receive any mental pictures and this frustrates him immensely. He is determined to 'see'. I have regressed him numerous times through the years and we have obtained a great deal of information about his past lives, but he continues to feel that he cannot really regress because he does not see pictures.

Regression is a way of getting to know yourself. Learn to be sensitive to subtle changes in your senses and in your body during the regression experiences. These changes are all ways of getting information. Perhaps you are trying to determine where you are in a past life. Maybe you have the sudden sensation of the warmth of the sun on your skin or a light breeze. Chances are that you are outdoors. Perhaps you become aware of a particular smell which is not appropriate to your physical surroundings. If, for instance, in the here and now you are in a large city and you are suddenly aware of smelling a barnyard during the regression, it is safe to assume that in the past life time you are in or near a barnyard and that there are horses or cattle around. Being sensitive to these subtle impressions helps to focus the mind on that particular lifetime and will encourage more vivid impressions and sensory input. It gets easier with each regression.

"What if I can't be regressed?" you ask. I have yet to meet a person who cannot be regressed. I have met many people who did not think they could be regressed. There have been those who did not believe in reincarnation, those who were violently opposed to the idea but willing to try to show that past-life memories did not exist, those who didn't believe one way or another, those who were convinced that they couldn't regress because no one had ever been able to hypnotize them. (But this is not conventional hypnosis per se). Every one of them regressed. You will, too.

There is very little about the regression experience which is critical. If you become uncomfortable, change positions. If you itch, scratch. If the telephone rings, you can relay information through whomever answers it. Just keep your eyes closed and after the interruption continue with the regression where you left off. I know one person who keeps a glass of tea and cigarettes at hand, and partakes as casually as if it were a normal social occasion, but with eyes closed.

You are in control during the regression session. You may terminate the session at any time by simply opening your eyes. If you terminate the session in this way, do affirm to yourself, "I will bring with me all information and impressions which will be of benefit to me, I will leave behind anything which might be detrimental to me in any way." The reason for ending the regression with these statements is that often this is all that is necessary to free your present self from undesirable feelings, fears, reactions and attitudes which have their roots in past life experiences.

During the regression, you are in control and may refuse to explore any experience which is disagreeable to you or which you choose to explore privately at another time. Just don't use that ability to ignore information which you need to think about and deal with.

There are many marvelous tapes on the market for guidance into relaxation states, subliminal conditioning and to provide a soothing musical background. In most circumstances, I enthusiastically endorse their use, but with this particular regression technique, we have found the tapes to be more of a distraction than a help. Music can often trigger associations or emotions which have nothing to do with the particular past life under scrutiny and can therefore 'muddy the waters'. As far as the relaxation tapes are concerned, while relaxation is initially used as an introduction into the regression experience, the state of physical relaxation is 'keyed' so that you may return to that relaxed state any time you desire to and remain alert, awake and aware, and rapidly progress beyond the need to use any type of induction for regression. Relying on a relaxation tape can interfere with this progression and promote an association of sleep or lessened awareness with the regression experience. Apart from regression, the relaxation and conditioning tapes are fun and beneficial to use.

I do not encourage joint regressions, i.e., two or more people regressing back to the same lifetime simultaneously, or joint psychic investigations of any type, until the people involved are proficient enough to recognize which impressions are from their own minds and which are from other sources. Often there is cross-feed (telepathy) between two people working at those levels of mind which can distort or cloud emotions and information. Just as two people looking at a physical object with their physical eyes will have differing perceptions and interpretations, the same is true on a psychic level. By the time a mild emotion for someone or something has been passed back and forth a time or two, a simple dislike can be distorted into a bitter hatred or a friendship into a grand passion.

Each person's mind-voice is as distinctive as his speaking voice. Until you can recognize the characteristics of your own mind-voice as opposed to that of another person, it is best to make your own regression experiences solo.

Please do not use alcohol or drugs before a regression. The effects of these substances on the mind can produce unnecessary complications during a regression, the least of which is a distorted experience and invalid information. At those levels of mind, alcohol and drugs diminish your control over the direction of the regression and you can end up by triggering highly traumatic responses without any mental defenses. In other instances, very trivial bits of information can seem to be terribly important, while important information can be missed. Experience has shown that often, after the regression, little or no clear perception of the experience is retained.

You should be in control of the regression experience at all times. The person directing you is present as an aid to help you focus your attention until such time as you can regress yourself. If that person attempts to take aggressive control of the regression or persists in asking leading questions, or is not conducting himself properly in some manner, terminate the session and refuse to work with him in the future.

Be honest with yourself. If you claim impressions which you do not experience or make up stories to impress your audience, you are the one who loses the chance for an exciting and valuable experience. Don't cheat yourself.

Last of all, relax. After a regression or two you will wonder how you possibly could have been tense or reluctant to experience something which is so informative and so much fun.

Chapter Three

The Regression Technique

To begin the regression have the person being regressed assume a comfortable position. Begin by directing the person through the following standard relaxation exercise. Speak in a normal conversational tone of voice.

"Close your eyes. Direct your awareness to your *eyelids*. (Pause for about 2-3 seconds.) Notice any muscles which may be tense. (Pause) Cause your eyelids to relax. Relax each muscle so that your eyelids become completely relaxed. (Pause)

Direct your awareness to your *scalp*. (Pause) Notice any muscles which may be tense. Especially notice the small muscles around the edge of the scalp. (Pause) Relax your scalp. Relax each muscle so that your scalp becomes completely relaxed. (Pause)

Direct your awareness to your *face*. (Pause)
Notice any muscles which may be tense. (Pause)
Allow the muscles of your face to become
completely relaxed. (Pause)

Direct your awareness to your *jaw*. Become aware
of the muscles which control your jaw. (Pause)
Allow your jaw to relax. Relax each muscle so
that your jaw is loose — completely relaxed.
(Pause)

Direct your awareness to your *neck*. Become
aware of the muscles which control your neck.
(Pause) Relax your neck. Relax each muscle. Relax each nerve. Relax each cell. Allow your neck
to become completely relaxed. (Pause)

Direct your awareness to your *hands*. (Pause)
Become aware of the many small muscles and
bones in your hands. (Pause) Relax your hands.
Allow each muscle, each nerve, each cell to
become completely relaxed. (Pause)

Direct your awareness to your *chest*, an area
containing muscles, organs, glands and nerves.
(Pause) Relax each muscle, each organ, each
gland, each nerve. Allow each cell to function in
a normal, rhythmic manner. Allow your chest to
become completely relaxed. (Pause)

Direct your awareness to your *abdomen*, an area
containing muscles, organs, glands and nerves.
(Pause) Relax each muscle, each organ, each
gland, each nerve. Allow each cell to function in
a normal rhythmic manner. Allow your abdomen

to completely relax. (Pause)

Direct your awareness to your *legs*. (Pause) Notice any muscles which may be tense. (Pause) Relax your legs. Allow your legs to become completely relaxed. (Pause)

Direct your awareness to your *feet*, an area of many small muscles and bones. (Pause) Notice any muscles which may be tense. (Pause) Relax your feet. Allow your feet to become completely relaxed. (Pause)

It is a wonderful feeling to be relaxed, a very natural and healthy state of being. Anytime you desire to return to this state of relaxation, all you have to do is take a deep breath and as you exhale, mentally repeat the word RELAX three times and you will become completely relaxed.

You are in complete control at every level of mind. You are relaxed but mentally alert and aware. Should you choose to terminate this session, you need only to open your eyes.

Should someone call you in case of danger or an emergency, you will immediately be alert and aware and fully oriented to the present time and place.

I may terminate this session by counting to you from 1 to 5, or touching you on either shoulder three times. At the count of 5, or when you feel my hand touch your shoulder for the third time, your eyes will open, you will be alert and refreshed.

You will bring with you from the regression experience everything which will be beneficial to
you in any way. You will leave behind everything which might be detrimental to you in
any way.

At this time I am going to direct you through
some mental exercises. Tell me when you have
completed each exercise. They will only take a
moment.

Become unaware of your *feet*. Cause your feet
to feel as if they do not belong to your body.
Tell me when you have done this. It will only
take a moment." (Pause)

Insist that the individual respond to you verbally as he
completes each exercise. Do not allow yourself to become
bogged down in this exercise. If the individual indicates
some difficulty, just tell them to 'play-like' or imagine that
their feet are no longer a part of their body. When there
has been a verbal response, continue.

"Good. Your feet now feel as if they do not
belong to your body.

Become unaware of your *legs*. Cause your legs to
feel as though they do not belong to your body.
It will only take a moment. Tell me when you
have done this. (Pause for response.) Good. Your
feet and legs now feel as though they do not
belong to your body.

Become unaware of your *abdomen*. Cause your
abdomen to feel as though it does not belong to

your body. It will only take a moment. Tell me
when you have done this. (Pause for response.)
All right, your feet, legs and abdomen feel as
though they do not belong to your body.

Become unaware of your *chest*. Cause your
chest to feel as though it does not belong to
your body. Tell me when you have done this.
It will only take a moment. (Pause for response.)
Good, your feet, legs, abdomen, and chest now
feel as if they do not belong to your body.

It is a wonderful feeling to be relaxed, a very
natural, healthy state of being.

Now quickly imagine that you are standing in
front of the building where you presently live. It
will only take a moment. Tell me as soon as you
are there. (Pause for response.) Good. Now briefly
describe the front of the building to me. Tell me
what you would see if you were physically standing in front of the building where you now live.
(Pause for a brief description.) What season of
the year is it? (Start with the season of year
named, substitute in the proper sequence in the
following exercise.) It's fall? Fine. Now imagine
that it is winter. It will only take a moment. Describe how the appearance of the building and
surrounding area differs in the winter. (Pause for
a brief response.)

Good. Now imagine that it is spring. Describe
how the appearance differs in the spring. (Pause
for a brief response.)

Good. Now imagine that it is summer. Describe
how the appearance differs in the summer. (Pause
for a brief response.)

Now, imagine that it is fall again."

When these preliminary exercises have been completed at
the first regression, it is not necessary to repeat them for
subsequent regressions. Simply tell the person to relax by
taking a deep breath and while exhaling to mentally repeat
the word RELAX three times. Then, begin at this point.

"Imagine that you are standing in front of the
door to your home. Imagine that you are opening the door. Imagine that the door opens into a
long tunnel and that you can see a light at the
end of the tunnel. I am going to count from 20
to 1. With each descending number imagine that
you are moving down the tunnel toward the light
and moving back through time to a lifetime you
lived previous to this one. At the count of 1 you
will step from the tunnel into the light, into a
lifetime which you lived previous to this one.

20 (Pause), 19 (Pause), 18, moving toward the
light back through time to a lifetime you lived
previous to this one. 17 (Pause), 16 (Pause), 15,
moving toward the light and back through time,
14 (Pause), 13 (Pause), 12. At the count of 1
you will be in a lifetime which you lived previous
to this one. 11 (Pause), 10 (Pause), 9, moving
down through the tunnel toward the light, back
to a lifetime you lived previous to this one, 8
(Pause), 7 (Pause), 6, back through time, 5 (Pause),
4 (Pause), 3. At the count of 1 you will step

from the tunnel into the light, into a lifetime which you lived previous to this one. 2 (Pause), 1. You are now in a lifetime which you lived previous to this one.

Mentally look out through your eyes and listen through your ears. Mentally look down at your feet. What are you wearing on your feet? (Pause for a response and then continue with the questioning.)

What are you wearing on your body?
About what age are you?
Are you male or female?
What is your name, the first name which comes to mind? Mentally look out through your eyes and listen through your ears. Where are you? Describe your surroundings.
What part of the world are you in?
Do you know what year or time period it is?
What does your mother look like?
How do you feel about her? Do you have a good relationship?
What does your father look like?
How do you feel about him?
Do you have any brothers or sisters?
Do you have any close friends?

Quickly scan one day in your life. It will only take a moment. How do you spend your time?

Move forward in time to the point where you are approximately 5 years older, about the age of _____. It will only take a moment. You will feel time passing around you like currents of

air or the pages flipping off a calendar. Tell me
as soon as you are there.

Mentally look out through your eyes and listen
through your ears. Where are you and what are
you doing?
Are you married?
Do you have children?
Do you believe in a Higher Power?
Do you belong to any formal religion?
How do you feel about your spiritual life?
Are you happy?

Quickly scan the next 10, 15, or 20 years (whatever is appropriate to the age they are at this
time in the regression). It will only take a moment. Tell me about any outstanding events or
accomplishments which you would like to share.

Is there anything you particularly want to do
that you have not been able to?

Is there anything that you have done of which
you feel particularly proud?

These are only sample questions to use as a guideline. You
will have to use your own judgement as to whether certain
questions are appropriate to the circumstances or if another
sequence is better. Also, these questions are meant to elicit
general information and will probably point up certain lines
of questioning appropriate to the person and the information which you will want to pursue.

At this time, direct the person into another past-lifetime.

"At this time, go back in time to a lifetime which you lived previous to this one. It will only take a moment. Tell me as soon as you are there. You will arrive at about age 12."

Continue with the same type of questions as in the previous lifetime. If time permits, you may want to visit still another lifetime in the same manner.

When you are ready to terminate the regression say:
"In a moment I will count from 1 to 5. At the count of 5 you will open your eyes in the here and now, feeling alert and refreshed. You will bring with you everything on every level which might be beneficial to you in any way. You will leave behind everything which might be detrimental to you in any way.

1 − 2 − 3, at the count of 5 you will be in your present lifetime as _____ _____, feeling refreshed and alert. 4 − 5, eyes open, feeling refreshed and alert."

Some Miscellaneous Information
During the relaxation exercise, some individuals may experience a feeling of warmth or a tingling sensation in the various areas of their body as their attention is directed to that area. This is perfectly normal. The warm feeling is due to increased circulation in that area caused by the focus of your attention. The tingling feeling is due to an increased awareness of the nervous systems in those areas. Don't be concerned if you didn't feel either of these sensations. That is perfectly normal too.

Another physical phenomena which may be noted to one degree or another throughout the regression is the rapid movement of the eyes underneath the lids, or a fluttering of the eyelids. This is REM, Rapid Eye Movement, and is a physical manifestation of the deep Alpha levels on which the person is mentally operating. This phenomena is also present during the dream sequence of sleep.

Immediately following the regression is a good time to make note of any additional details which the person may remember but didn't mention during the regression. It is also important to note down anyone who was recognized during the regression as being someone known in this present lifetime.

Do not be disturbed if initially, directly after the regression, you feel a little uncomfortable or embarrassed as if you had made the whole thing up. This is not uncommon, but the feeling rapidly fades as spontaneous memories begin to occur.

The first regression experience is basically intended to elicit general information and set the scene for later, more detailed regressions. If desired, specific lifetimes may be revisited by stating, "You will be in the lifetime you lived as _____." If no name was remembered, the lifetime may be identified by time period, location, or any other outstanding, identifying feature.

If there is an attraction to a certain time period or locale, you may direct a person there by saying, "You will be in any lifetime you may have lived during _____ or in _____." Always use the phrase 'may have lived'. The attraction may exist for reasons other than past lives. There is no reason to subject the subconscious to the confusion of being told to remember a lifetime which never happened.

One very rewarding approach to subsequent regressions is to direct the individual to regress back to "the lifetime which is most significant to you today in your lifetime as _____ _____".

If the person being regressed has a specific problem he or she wants to investigate, direct the individual to go "to the point in time where this problem had its origin". This should not be done until the individual has had some regression experiences and feels comfortable with the technique. It should be done only with the understanding that if the problem is very traumatic in this lifetime, it has the potential of being even more so at its point of origin. Reassure the individual often during the regression that "you are physically here and now and this is simply an exercise in remembering. There is no need for you to experience distress of any kind on any level." Encourage the person to disassociate himself from the situation and observe as if watching a movie or television.

It is seldom necessary to be this aggressive in looking for origins of problems, as the answers will usually surface during the course of several regressions. After a person has had a few regression experiences and is able to do self-directed regressions, finding the origins of problems is much simpler. Self-directed regressions are the most desirable method for exploring situations of this nature. There is a protective mechanism within the mind which protects an individual from forcing his own recall into areas that he is not ready to deal with or cannot handle for some reason.

If, during the course of a regression, you direct someone to move ahead a few years in that lifetime and the person arrives in a 'blank' spot with no sensory input, it is probably after the death experience. Just direct the individual back into another lifetime. (Methods for exploring the death experiences are covered in a later chapter.)

After you have gained some confidence and feel comfortable conducting a regression, you may find that there are modifications which are appropriate for your circumstances and the people you are working with. You may find a different type or pattern of questions easier to work with. Feel free to change your approach as circumstances dictate. The exact method is not sacred. The only parts of the technique which are important and should not be changed are those statements establishing the awareness and control of the person being regressed and the positive statements used in terminating the session. You do have a duty to use the technique in a careful, thoughtful and responsible manner.

During a regression, especially the first one, it is not unusual for there to be no response to certain questions; name, age, date, locale, etc. If no response is elicited to one or more of these questions just say, "That's all right," and move on. As with any new experience, it may take a time or two to become proficient at recalling information. As proficiency builds, some individuals may be able to remember such detailed information as exact birthdate and time in some of the more recent lifetimes. Astrological birth charts for past lifetimes often provide interesting insight into the present lifetime.

Past-life regression is just one more step on the path to self-awareness. When the day comes that being regressed or directing a regression is no longer fresh and exciting and no new information of any real value is being obtained, move on. Later you will probably find that occasionally a need for additional information or some other reason will occur which will spark the desire for further regressions. Use it as you would use a necessary tool for any job.

Chapter Four

Sample Regressions

The following material is taken from two separate regressions which were done on the same individual several weeks apart. The first lifetime revisited was the very first regression experience both for the person being regressed and the person directing the regression. They were working with written instructions as presented in the previous chapter.

I have combined these two regressions into one simple regression to illustrate how to move from one lifetime to another, how to deal with various situations which might occur, and how to adapt the questions to the information received when it becomes impractical to follow the standard line of questioning.

These two examples were chosen specifically because of the dramatic content and the unexpected and difficult situations which occurred during the regressions. As you will see, they were handled successfully by two inexperienced people by simply following the written instructions.

Some of the situations which occurred: no impressions in answer to certain questions, popping into the middle of a potentially disturbing scenario, finding the very traumatic reason for an existing phobia, and obtaining a great deal of meaningful information for both participants.

For clarity I have used 'Q' to designate the dialogue of the person directing the regression and 'A' to designate the dialogue of the person being regressed. Both parties were in their early thirties at the time of the regressions. 'A' was a housewife married to 'Q', an engineer.

Q: . . . 2, 1. You are now in a lifetime which you lived previous to this one. Mentally look out through your eyes and listen through your ears. Mentally look down at your feet. What do you have on your feet?

A: I don't see anything. But, my feet do feel funny.

Q: What do you mean by funny?

A: Well, they feel bare, but like I'm standing in something. I know, it feels like I'm standing in water with mud squishing up between my toes.

Q: Where are you?

A: I'm wading in the water.

Q: Why are you in the water? How are you dressed?

A: I feel like I have on a loose shirt and some type of skirt. The skirt is tucked up somehow to keep it out of the water. I'm very tired. My back hurts. I'm bending over putting something in the water.

(At first, most of her information came through the means of physical feelings.)

Q: Mentally look out through your eyes and listen through your ears. Where are you and what are you doing?

A: Oh, I see something. I'm putting little green plants into the mud. I think it's rice. Yes, I'm planting rice. I'm Chinese.

Q: Mentally look around. Are there other people with you?

A: Yes, there is an older man working in the field with me.

Q: Who is he?

A: My husband.

Q: Are you female, then?

A: Yes.

Q: About what age are you?

A: I don't know.

Q: Are you young, middle-aged, or old?

(Note that he gives her a choice and this elicits an answer.)

A: I feel young, very young. Maybe just barely teenaged.

Q: How old is your husband?

A: Much older than me. About 30 at least.

Q: What is your name — the first name which comes to mind?

A: I don't know. I don't get an impression of any name.

Q: When your husband talks to you, what does he call you?

(This was a good approach to use to encourage an answer without using undue pressure.)

A: Sometimes he calls me 'Woman-child' or 'Young Wife'. I'm not sure that I have a real name.

Q: What about your parents? Describe your mother to me.

A: I think my parents died when I was very young. My impressions of them are very vague and shadowy.

Q: Who raised you?

A: At first I think that several people in our little village took turns feeding me. Then I went to live with an old woman. She let me live with her because she wanted someone to do her work. Then she sold me.

Q: Why did she do that?

A: She didn't like me and I didn't like her. She was ill-tempered and stingy. She thought I ate too much. Orphan females were considered worthless but the man was willing to pay her a lot of rice and other things for me.

Q: Who was the man who bought you?

A: My husband. His wife had died in childbirth. He needed someone to help him in the rice fields. The other unmarried girls in the village were either too young or too old.

Q: Do you like your husband?

A: Yes. He is a very good man. He is kind to me. I work hard in the fields with him. He is a good farmer. He raises good crops. We have plenty to eat and some to sell. I have warm clothes for winter.

Q: Do you have any children?

A: Yes. I have given him a son. He is very pleased with me.

Q: Where do you live?

(Here the pride in her voice was unmistakable — almost a smug superiority. Her answer proved the old saying, 'Rich is relative'.)

A: We have the grandest house in the village. We have TWO rooms and a small courtyard. We have one room for cooking and working and another room for sleeping. We have mats on the floor woven from straw and reeds. We have two stools for sitting. We have thick mats for sleeping and warm covers. No one else in the village has such a large house. We have two rooms!

Q: At this time, go to the point in time where you are about one year older. It will only take a moment. Tell me as soon as you are there. You will feel time passing around you like currents of air or pages flipping off a calendar.

(At this point she began breathing rapidly and moaning and straining. You could actually see the muscles contracting in her abdomen.)

A: Oh! Oh! I'm having a baby. It hurts.

Q: Detach yourself from this. Physically you are in the here and now. This is simply an exercise in remembering. There is no need for you to feel pain, discomfort or distress on any level. You are just remembering something which happened a long time ago. Step back and watch. Don't be a part of it.

A: All right. It's okay now.

Q: Do you want to continue?

A: Yes, it's okay now. (Smiling) It was just unexpected and I forgot I wasn't really there. I'm detached now.

Q: Good. We'd have a hard time explaining a newborn Chinese infant.

A: That's the truth. (Laughing) I'm fine now, let's go on.

Q: Okay. Go to the point in time which is one day after the birth of your child. It will only take a moment. Tell me when you are there.

(This situation of physical involvement was quite unusual. Q handled it just right in a calm, matter-of-fact manner with a sense of humor. His attitude communicated itself to A and she handled it well. Both look back on the incident with amusement. Since she tended to gain a great deal of her information through physical sensations and a close emotional identification with her past selves, Q made it a point in subsequent regressions to remind her frequently that she was physically in the here and now, and just remembering the past. A made a point of keeping herself detached when such situations seemed probable. Gradually she obtained more and more of her information through 'seeing' and 'knowing' and less through feeling.)

A: Okay. I'm there.

Q: Mentally look out through your eyes and listen through your ears. Where are you and what are you doing?

A: I am in our sleeping room with the baby. My husband and firstborn son are with me. My husband is very pleased. Now he has two sons. He calls me 'Good

Wife' and tells me to stay at home today. Then he leaves.

Q: Where is he going?

A: To the fields. It is rice planting time again. This will be two days he has worked alone. He needs me but I am tired. I will rest today and help him tomorrow. He is very kind to me.

Q: What else do you do besides raise rice?

A: We raise vegetables and we have two pigs. I take care of the house and cook the meals. Sometimes I weave mats and baskets and sandals out of reeds, grass and rice straw.

Q: Do you have any close friends?

A: No, not really. My husband has friends. Mostly we just work.

Q: What does your husband do with the rice?

A: We store some for food and seed. The rest he takes to a market town and sells or trades for things we need — tools, food, material for clothes, tea. We drink tea almost every day. Sometimes he brings me a treat — a small cake of sugar or a piece of candied ginger. He says that some day he will buy me a singing bird in a cage which he has seen in the market.

(It seemed obvious at this point that this probably was not going to be a lifetime to pursue in any depth, so it was time to move on.)

Q: All right. At this time, scan the next 20 years. Tell me of any outstanding events or accomplishments. It will only take a few moments. Tell me when you are there.

A: Okay, I'm there. I gave my husband five sons. The three eldest are married and have children. As our sons got old enough to work in the fields, my husband bought more land with the coins he had saved. When the fifth son was born he bought me a singing bird in a cage. He named me 'Fruitful Wife'. He died three years ago. Our sons take care of me.

Q: What do you do with your time?

A: I teach the sons' wives how to be good wives. I tell them what to do. I teach my grandchildren to be good, obedient children. Right now, my chest hurts and I cough all of the time. I don't think I am going to get well.

Q: How do you feel about your life?

A: I was a good wife. I worked hard and gave my husband five sons. I have had a good life.

Q: At this time, go back to a lifetime which you lived previous to this one. It will only take a moment. Tell me as soon as you are there. You will arrive at about age 12.

(Age 12 is used as a starting point because at that age the person is old enough to be pretty well aware of what is going on around them on a broader scale than a younger child. It also gives a good reference point for progressing the person to various periods of their lives.)

A: Okay, I'm there.

Q: Mentally look out through your eyes and listen through your ears. Look down at your feet. What do you have on your feet?

A: Nothing. I'm barefooted and my feet are cold.

Q: Why are your feet cold?

A: It is winter and I don't have my shoes on.

Q: What do you have on your body?

A: Britches and a shirt — homespun.

Q: Why are you cold?

A: I was in a hurry to go to the outhouse.

Q: Are you male or female?

A: Male.

Q: About what age are you?

A: 12.

Q: What is your name?

A: Benjamin. Little Ben is what they call me.

Q: Don't you have a chamber pot in your house?

A: Them what uses 'em hast ta empty 'em. I ain't goin' to get stuck with that.

Q: Where do you live?

A: With my family.

Q: Where is that? Do you know what part of the world?

A: Course I do. The Louisiana Purchase. (Except he pronounced it Lou-ess-z-anner) The part they call Arkansas.

Q: Tell me about your family.

A: Well, there's Ma and Pa and eleven of us kids.

Q: Tell me about your parents.

A: Pa is about the best shot around. He knows all about the woods and where to find the animals. Seems like the fish just come beggin' to be caught by him. He doesn't like farming much but he does it real careful like, like he does everything. Pa is probably the most smartest man around. He knows readin' and writin' and figgurin'. You don't put nothing over on him. He ain't mean but he shore is strict. He can shore warm your britches if you don't mind.

Q: What does he look like?

A: He's middlin' tall. Has brown hair and brown eyes. He's got whiskers but Ma makes him keep them trimmed up. She don't like them much past his chin. He growls about it but he does it to please her. She keeps his hair all trimmed up too. Says it's cleaner. She's a demon for clean.

Q: Tell me about your mother.

A: She's most as tall as Pa. She has lots of shiny brown hair that she skins back into a big knot with big bone pins that belonged to her ma. She gets kinda mad sometimes because it keeps coming loose and curling round her face. Pa teases her about it. Her eyes are kinda greeny-grey. She works hard. Seems like she is always scrubbing something or someone. Pa says it's a good thing we live close to the creek or we'd need another eleven kids to tote water. Ma says she ain't going to raise a passel of dirty heathens just cos we live in the middle of heathenland. She don't take no foolishness off nobody. But mostly she's a smiley kinda person. She likes the woods and animals and pretty leaves and flowers.

Q: What about your brothers and sisters?

A: William, he's the oldest. He's been gone most a year and a half now.

Q: What happened to him?

A: Pa said he had a wanderin' foot and he was a man. He was 17. Pa let him go with some trappers who were headed up north. Wish I coulda gone. I'd like to git away from all these girls.

Q: Your sisters?

A: Yes! Amanda and Abigail mostly. They's both older than me. Lordy, I hope they git married soon. They're always giggling and makin' mooney eyes at them Mueller boys that keep coming around. When they aren't doing that they're ordering me around or teasing me. Then there's the twins, Martha and Mary. They's younger than me by two years. Ma named them after them sisters in the Bible. They's always tagging around after me. Don't give me no peace. And where they go, John, who's a year younger than them, goes. Sarah ain't too bad. She's only 7 but she's a lot like Ma. She's always playing mama to Matthew who's a year younger than her and Henry who's three and baby Elizabeth who ain't a year yet. She mostly leaves me alone.

Q: What do you do with your days?

A: I help Pa with the crops and chop wood and carry

water from the creek for Ma. I spend half the day carrying water. Sometimes me and Pa go hunting or fishing. I like that best. Pa, too. But he says we got to do what's most needful first. Crops have to be tended at the proper time. Them squirrels and deer and fish will wait but crops won't. Mostly I like to go roaming the hills by myself. Don't get to do that much.

Q: Why not?

A: Ma worries about Indians. I ain't never seen none. She's more worrisome since Will went and we ain't heard no word of him. I reckon she's worried I'll go off too.

Q: Do you go to school at all?

A: Ain't no school around but Ma and Pa teach us. They both set quite a store by book learning. My Ma knows how to read and write. During the winter time they teach us readin' from the Bible. Pa fixed a shaller box with wet sand where we do our letters with a twig. Come Sundays Ma makes us kids take turns readin' from the Bible. I like to read the 'begats'. I know the names of the numbers. Some of them ole names are kinda hard but I kin mumble a bit on them and come out right strong with how long they lived and all them begats. Them fellers shore did live a long time. Ma makes us do sums too. Says she ain't gonna raise no bunch of ignorant heathens.

Q: Do you know what the date is, or at least the year?

A: Yep. Ma keeps track of the days. Says we ain't going to be like the heathens who only know the change of the seasons. I'd shore like to meet some of them heathens some time. They sound right interesting. Let's see now. I don't remember the count of the days, but the month is December and the year is 1810.

Q: At this time, move forward in time about one year. To the point in time where you are about one year older. It will only take a moment. Tell me as soon as you are there.

A: Okay.

Q: Mentally look out through your eyes and listen through your ears. Where are you and what are you doing?

A: I'm at home. I'm getting my warm things on to go out. I told Ma and Pa that I'm going hunting and looking. This time a year they don't ask a lot of questions.

Q: What time of year is it?

A: Winter. December, 1811.

Q: Where are you going? Are you doing something you're not supposed to?

A: Not really. I got me a secret. I want to keep it a secret as long as I can. Don't often get to have a secret with all them kids around. I'll show Pa one of these days, but I want to look it out right proper for myself before I do.

Q: What is the secret?

A: I found me a big ole cave, or maybe two, during the fall when I was follerin' a deer. I ain't been in past the first little bit of one. Too dark. I fixed me some torches and left there. I'm gonna look it out proper today.

Q: Okay. Move ahead to your arrival at the cave. It will only take a moment. Tell me when you are there.

A: Okay.

Q: Mentally look out through your eyes and listen through your ears. Where are you and what are you doing?

A: I brought Pa's flint and steel and tinder box to set me a fire. It's cold but I need the fire anyways to light the torches. I'm gonna set a spell and warm up before I go in. It's kinda scary and strange looking. I hope they ain't no bears denned up in there. That's the trouble with caves in winter. Snakes in summer, bears in winter.

Q: Tell me about the cave.

A: I wish Pa were here. It ain't like a regular cave where there's a hole in the side of a cliff or hill. It's hard to describe. They's kinda of a overhang with big ole slabs of rock angling all which-a-ways. Scary looking.

(Up until this point it was obvious that A had been closely identifying with Benjamin, falling into some of his speech patterns very naturally. You might say that she had become Benjamin. This was fine up until Benjamin arrived at the cave. Then A began to get restless, her pattern of breathing changed, the tone of her voice changed, and she began clenching and unclenching her hands. Q had been watching this closely and was quick to pick up on the fact that he needed to intervene.)

Q: Are you getting a little nervous about this?

A: Yes. I feel uneasy. I need to disassociate myself from Benjamin. Something bad is going to happen.

Q: Would you like to stop or go on to something else?

A: No. I want to see what happens. I think it is going to be very important for me to know.

Q: Okay. Just detach yourself and step back and observe what happens. Remember that this is an exercise in remembering. Whatever happened, happened a long time ago. There is no need for you to feel distress of any kind on any level. Go ahead when you are ready.

A: Okay, here goes. Benjamin lights one of the torches in the little fire he has built. He has made several from tree bark and dried grass. He takes them all with him, planning to light one from another as he needs them. He is pretty nervous about going into the cave but he is excited too, and determined to go. There are lots of slabs of rock that he has to crawl over and around and pick a path through. It seems to be limestone mostly. He keeps stopping and smelling the air to see if he can smell bear or a snake den. He goes deeper into the cave. The torch doesn't give much light. He is afraid, too. He moves slowly, looking all around him very carefully. Something doesn't feel quite right. He doesn't know what. He just feels like he really shouldn't be there. He thinks maybe he'll go tell his Pa about the cave and come back later with him. He feels kind of ashamed for being afraid. He is standing still, trying to make up his mind what to do. Something is wrong. Everything feels shakey. The ground is shaking. It's an earthquake. Benjamin is trying to run for the entrance. It's like trying to run on jello. He doesn't understand what is happening. He keeps falling down. There are rocks falling in the cave.

Q: Relax. Keep yourself detached. Just observe. You are only remembering something which happened a long time ago.

A: Yes, I'm all right. I'm a little shakey, but I'm all right. But Benjamin — he's not far from the entrance when he falls and rolls over onto his back. A huge slab of rock comes crashing down just above him.

Q: Did it kill him?

A: No. It would have been better if it had. He's trapped. The rock is wedged in just a few inches from his face. His feet are caught somehow. He can't turn over or move. There are other rocks all around him. It's like a stone coffin. The ground has stopped shaking. There is dust in the air and little rocks are still falling. Then it gets very quiet. Benjamin can see a little daylight through the cracks between the rocks, or maybe it's the torch still burning. He tries to stay calm and see if there is any way he can free himself. He can't move. He can just barely see the slab of rock just above his face. He wants to turn over so he can't see it. There just isn't enough room. Even if there was his feet are caught. He just wants to turn onto his stomach so much. He feels like it would be safer somehow, or could at least pretend the rock wasn't there. He tries so hard to be strong and calm but the panic starts building inside and just keeps on until it overwhelms him. He starts screaming and crying and trying to push against the rocks but it's like being in a strait-jacket. He screams and screams and just goes wild. Poor little boy. He has never been so afraid of anything.

Q: Are you all right?

A: Yes. It bothers me some. I know the panic he is feeling. I know how helpless and afraid he feels. But it is answering some questions for me. I want to go ahead. Don't be upset if I cry. It's as much relief as anything.

Q: Yes, I understand. Just stay as detached as possible. You are just remembering. It's not happening now.

A: Yes, I know. Okay. It gets dark. Benjamin is exhausted. He sleeps for awhile but awakens very cold. He thinks maybe his father will come and find him and he calms himself with that thought for awhile. But he knows that the possibility of his father being able to track him is unlikely. He knows, too, that even if his father found him the slab of rock is too big to move. He finally accepts that he is going to die there. Every time he tries to move he panics again. He screams and cries and tries to claw the rock. He tries to think of ways to kill himself. He is so angry. He hopes maybe it will get cold enough to freeze him to death. He keeps on having bouts of panic and screaming. Each time he gets a little weaker and begins to lose touch with reality. This goes on for two days. Finally he doesn't know who he is or where he is. He is lost in a fog of terror and panic and wanting to be free. Toward morning of the third day, something snaps and everything goes blank for a moment. Then he is suddenly standing in front of the cave. He is dazed and confused. It takes a few minutes for him to realize that he is dead. I want to quit now.

Q: Okay. In a moment I will count from 1 to 5. At the count of 5 you will open your eyes in the here and now, feeling alert and refreshed. You will bring with you everything on every level from this experience which might be beneficial to you in any way. You will leave behind everything which might be detrimental to you in any way. 1 − 2 − 3 . . . .

While the second lifetime was more dramatic, A gained a great deal more information from the first lifetime than may be immediately apparent. First, from the viewpoint of the mechanics of regressing, she gained an understanding of her tendency to strongly identify with past-life personalities through physical feelings and emotions. After the experience of landing in the middle of childbirth, she learned to become more of an observer and she also learned to be somewhat intuitive about knowing when she was coming into a situation which might prove unpleasant.

A recognized the older Chinese man she was married to as her present husband, Q. Though the Chinese husband and wife worked side by side in the fields, and she presented him with five sons, because of the wide age difference there was a certain amount of a father-child attitude in their relationship. In their present marriage, A and Q have very much a relationship of equals. Q is a year older than A. Not often, but often enough to be of note to A, Q unconsciously takes a fatherly attitude toward her which "drives her up the wall", in her words. It is a very minor thing in their overall relationship, but now A understands that it comes not only from the culture in which they were last husband and wife, but also from the great age difference (17 − 20 years) in that lifetime.

The experience was important for Q for several reasons. From the viewpoint of directing a regression, Q learned how easily a calm, matter-of-fact approach can direct someone away from a disturbing situation and the importance of being observant. The experience also triggered his own memories of that lifetime and helped him to be aware of situations which prompted his fatherly reaction to A and avoid that reaction.

A and Q both had a good laugh about their five sons in that lifetime. Before they married in this present lifetime they had discussed the question of children and had decided on five — girls! They settled for less.

The second lifetime was extremely significant for A. It brought her the answer to a lifelong problem. She had struggled with severe claustrophobia all of her life. Such minor things as someone taking hold of her wrists, or having a problem pulling a snug blouse over her head could cause a feeling of panic. She grew up with nightmares of being buried alive. She never felt safe or comfortable sleeping any way but on her stomach with her feet outside the cover. Tight spaces of any kind made her uncomfortable. It was difficult for her to control her panic in even large caves though they held a fascination for her. She could never sleep in a bunk bed and couldn't bear to be zipped up in a sleeping bag. There were times that even making love with her husband threw her into panic. When she had her first baby, the main thought that terrified her was the possibility of having her hands strapped down in the delivery room, which was a common practice then. She needed repeated assurance from the doctor that he would not forget when the time came. Having x-rays was an ordeal — being positioned on her back with the equipment overhead. Putting anything over her face, a mask for anesthesia or a Halloween mask, could cause complete loss of control

She had found reasons for part of the claustrophobia in other past-lives and had gotten over a great deal of it before the Benjamin regression. However, there still remained a deep, traumatic fear of being shut in a space similar to a coffin or grave. Even more frightening to her was the great unknown something which lay behind the fear.

Several months prior to this regression, her husband was working on his car and asked for her assistance. This called for her to slide under the car on her back and hold a part in place. She slid under and was feeling very uncomfortable but managing to control her fear by concentrating on the part she was holding. Suddenly her husband changed position and put his feet across hers and shut off the space along the side of the car. She glanced up at the bottom of the car and lost control. She managed to slide out but she was crying and shaking, feeling anger, wanting to scream and claw and run. There was a feeling of the most complete terror she had ever known and a total loss of control. It was a profoundly traumatic experience.

Unwittingly, she and her husband had recreated a very similar situation to the one she had experienced as Benjamin. As she re-lived the experience as Benjamin, even though she detached herself emotionally from the situation, she knew exactly the emotions Benjamin felt, recognized them as twins to the indescribable fear and panic which had haunted her life. More important, the great and terrifying unknown which had been behind the fear was now revealed.

The immediate relief of knowing was tremendous. In following days A replayed the sequence over and over in her mind, releasing more of the emotions each time, and gaining a greater sense of freedom. A still dislikes being in tight situations, but 'dislike' is the key word. No longer do they cause fear or panic.

An interesting footnote: upon checking records, we found that in December, 1811, a massive earthquake with its epicenter somewhere around New Madrid, MO. (close to the north-eastern corner of Arkansas) shook an area of approximately 40,000 sq. miles. From a later, more detailed description of the caves, it is possible that the locale may have been Devil's Den Cave and the Devil's Ice Box, located about halfway between Fayetteville and Ft. Smith, but until A has visited there, that remains speculation.

Q handled this regression very well, immediately recognizing the first signs of agitation, giving A the choice as to whether or not to continue, then giving her positive and supportive reinforcement along the way.

The contrast between the detail and quality of information obtained in the two regressions is striking. A's first regression was a fairly typical first experience in that not a great deal of detail was remembered. The things which were easily recalled were the things which were most significant to the young wife: two rooms, five sons, and a bird in a cage.

Later, after A had regressed several times, it was much easier to recall more detailed information.

Look back over the past few years of your life. Which are the days you remember? Chances are very slight that you will remember the ordinary days. The specific days which are easily recalled are the days when something unusual happened: a particularly happy event, something frustrating or irritating, something sad or tragic, a birth, a death, a birthday or anniversary, an old friend heard from, a wedding, a divorce, an illness or an accident. The same is true of past lives. That is why sometimes it seems that past lives were more exciting and dramatic than present lives. You just don't remember much about the ordinary or boring days.

If you doubt that, make a list of the specific events and days you remember since childhood. Look at the list as if you were living another life sometime in the future and regressing back to this one. Considering just the events on the list you have made, doesn't this life time seem a little more exciting and dramatic than it really is? I mention this to help you put your regression experiences and those of others into the proper perspective. Remember, also, that we have lived many ordinary lives where even the unusual events were somewhat ordinary.

The following regression was conducted during the very early days of our work with the technique. The subject did not believe in reincarnation and did not want to believe, but was very willing and cooperative in participating in the experiment. B indicates the person being regressed, H the person directing the regression.

H: . . . you are now in a liftetime you lived previous to this one. . .

B: I have the impression of a gingham dress. The colors are purple amd orange. I have on a white apron with ruffles.

H: What age are you?

B: About 4.

H: What is your name?

B: Eliza.

H: Where do you live?

B: It's like in the country, but not country. The houses are far apart but close to the town.

H: Go to a point in time where you are about five years older, about nine years old. It will only take a moment; tell me when you're there.

B: I'm there.

H: Mentally look out through your eyes and listen through your ears. Where are you and what are you doing?

B: I hear the school bell. I have on a dark green dress but no apron. I have long black cotton stockings and bloomers with lace and ruffles.

H: Are you going to school?

B: No. I'm waiting for my brothers to come home. They

are coming. I see them waving.

H: What are their names?

B: Ezra and Jeremiah. My name is Mary Eliza.

H: How are they dressed?

B: Breeches and shirts.

H: Where do you live? What part of the world?

B: Kentucky.

H: Describe your mother to me.

B: No impression .

H: Describe your father to me.

B: No impression.

H: Go to a point in time where you are about five years older, about age fourteen. Tell me as soon as you are there.

B: I'm there.

H: Mentally look out through your eyes and listen through your ears. Where are you and what are you doing?

B: I'm sitting under some trees by a lake. There is an older man with me. I like him. He is smoking a long-stemmed pipe. He is bald on top but has long grey hair around the sides.

H: Who is he?

B: He may be my father.

(Beginning at this point, she answered every question with 'no impression' though it was fairly obvious that she was remembering a great deal of information. She did indicate her willingness to continue with another lifetime.)

H: You are now in a lifetime you lived previous to this one . . .

B: I'm skating. It's winter; very, very cold. December.

H: What is your name?

B: Katrine.

H: What age are you?

B: 9.

H: Where do you live?

B: Amsterdam.
H: What year is it?
B: I don't know.
H: Go to the time when you are about six months older.
B: The tulips and other flowers are in bloom. I have a
     beautiful dark red velvet dress with white lace and
     I'm wearing white hose.

(At this point, she began to speak with a marked German
type accent and there was an unusual rhythm to her speech.)

B: Papa has brought me wooden shoes. Ja. Wooden shoes
     like the peasants wear, but painted with flowers.
H: Tell me about your father.
B: Papa is a big man. Papa is handsome. He owns many
     fine restaurants. He is rich.
H: Tell me about your mother.
B: I have no mother.
H: Do you have any brothers or sisters?
B: Nein. No brothers. No sisters.
H: Go forward in time about six years, to the time when
     you are about fifteen. It will only take a moment.
     Tell me when you are there.
B: Ja.
H: Where are you and what are you doing?
B: In Amsterdam. I am flirting with the boys. Ja, I have
     many boy friends.
H: Do you have a special friend?
B: Ja freilich (yes, truly). Hans is my special boy friend.
     He is very handsome. He likes me, too. Ja. He is 19.
H: Are you going to marry Hans?
B: Ja. Nein — not yet. Papa say we must wait two years.
H: Move forward in time two years, to the time when
     you are about seventeen years old.
B: Ja. Hans still here. We are to marry. I have many beau-
     tiful dresses. My wedding dress is black (?) velvet with
     much lace. There are many important people here.

They are all beautiful. Papa says everyone is beautiful on a wedding day.
Here B indicated her desire to terminate the session. She was disturbed that she had gotten any impressions at all and extremely disturbed about the accent, speech patterns and foreign words. She said they just came out of her mouth. She volunteered that Katrine could probably speak English but German was her native tongue. She said that Katrine and her father had gone to Amsterdam from Germany after her mother had died when Katrine was very young. B then declined to discuss the experience further and never expressed a desire for a subsequent regression.

For those of you interested in more esoteric directions, the following regression will be of interest. The individual being regressed had shown a variety of marked psychic abilities on a number of occasions, but had very mixed and confused feelings about using them in any way which might bring attention. Having been regressed many times, the person was very much at ease with the technique and needed only limited direction. The questions did not follow the standard pattern as the person was in search of some very specific information. The first lifetime took place in Egypt, the second in Tibet. Z is directed by C.

C: Where are you?
Z: Sitting at a table watching a large green stone, an emerald, I think. A tiny hole has been drilled through the center and a fine gold wire passed through. It is anchored on each end horizontally so that the gem is suspended. I am causing the gem to turn, making it spin very fast with my mind. I enjoy the feeling of power it gives me.
C: Where did you learn to do this?
Z: I had the knowledge in a past lifetime and was caused

to remember it.

C: For what purpose?

Z: The record was written on the day of my birth. (Meaning his astrological birth chart) I was forced to remember. They tell me I shall need these abilities in this lifetime.

C: The ability to spin an object?

Z: I was only playing with the gem. I like to watch the fire as it spins and reflects the light. I like to concentrate on it and let it take me out of myself. I can move many things. It doesn't matter how large they are. It doesn't matter whether they are solid or liquid or vaporous — whether animate or inanimate.

C: Can you also move something non-physical; that is, can you move or shape thoughts and events?

Z: Yes. I wouldn't. There is too much I need to learn. But I would like to forget it all. They are always testing me instead of teaching me. There are so many coming into my mind all the time. They never leave me alone. Do this, do that.

C: When you were taught how to regain your abilities, do you remember how it was done, what you were told?

Z: Yes. Similar to what we're doing now but with other techniques I cannot tell.

C: Why?

Z: It was a vow I made to my first teachers. They said it would only trouble those who did not know what to do with the knowledge. Those that know what to do with the knowledge know how to get it. Besides, I have not finished. They tell me here that there is a final test. They also promise that after this test I will be free to guide my own life and make the decisions of how and when to use my mind.

C: When will the test be? What kind of test?

Z: It will be soon, very soon. I do not know what the test will be. I cannot think how else they could test me. I want it to be done and finished. I should have no cause to fear it, and yet I feel a sense of something evil in the air.

C: Can you find the source of the evil?

Z: No. I have looked within myself. I have done no one hurt or harm. I have not desired or taken that which belongs to another. I have taken no life. I have not spoken evil of another. I have not abused mind or body. I have not spoken of any of the sacred mysteries. I can find no evil within me unless it is evil to desire freedom, or want privacy in my mind, or sometimes desire to be free of this life.

C: Perhaps the evil is within someone else. Have you looked?

Z: I will not do to another what I so much dislike done to me. No, if there is evil afoot, I will meet it and conquer it. I have no need to fear becoming complete.

C: What is your name and age?

Z: Amman. I am 15.

C: Who were the first teachers you spoke of — the ones who taught you how to regain your abilities?

Z: My parents and a priest from one of the temples near our home.

C: Did they bring you here?

Z: No. These priests appeared at our home when I was about ten and said that it was written that I belonged to them. My parents did not want me to come, but they had no choice.

C: Why didn't they want you to come to this temple?

Z: I guess because I was so young. They told me to remain true to my vow and listen to the voice within me which tells me right from wrong. I have tried to do that, even though many temptations have been offered.

C: How have you been tempted?

Z: By the priests here. I knew that they were testing me to see if I could be persuaded to use my abilities for evil. I have resisted though I have been offered much. Actually there was no real temptation. Sometimes I think that they are not very intelligent, or don't think that I am. They know that I cannot be bribed, but I know that there would have been no payment. They would have just sent me from the temple. But I don't understand why this final test should plant the seed of fear within my mind.

C: Go to the time of the final test.

Z: For three days of preparation, I drink no water and eat no food. No cloth is allowed to touch my body. I stand in one place, praying and sending my soul forth to look and see and search to know if I have forgotten that which I should remember or if there is evil within me in some dark corner of my soul that I have not seen. I find only a question — why must we meet the gods in some dark foreboding place? Are they not on the banks of the river, in the green fields, in the sunlit desert? A strange question. Why should it occur to me? I would ask the priests but I am forbidden to speak until the final test is over. They won't even tell me what the test is. They say I will know when the time comes.

At dawn on the fourth day the priests come. They wash my body with water and anoint it with sacred oils. They spread the oil with small cloth pads and smile as they tell me it is a sacred oil, a mystery from the far past which must not touch their skins.

Why am I afraid? What have I to fear?

Now they lead me to a chamber far beneath the temple. My body trembles from the lack of food and

water — and from fear. This chamber is a cold, dark
place — a place of death. There is no warmth or life
here as I expected. There is evil here. Is it my fear?
I feel strange. My skin burns. My limbs are weak.
They give me one swallow of potion, they say to aid
me on my way. Where? It tastes strange and acid on
my tongue.

I am alone now. I am too weak to stand or sit. I
still do not understand the test. I try to leave my
body, but my mind is clouded. I cannot leave my
body and I am afraid. I understand the evil now. The
fear is not my fear. The fear is that of the priests.
They fear me and the evil is within them. They could
not control me or subvert me to their evil will. The
sacred oil was poison, the potion a drug to cloud my
mind.

Gods of Egypt — why have you allowed this? I
served you with all my heart. I deny you as you deny
me! I curse all those who serve within this temple! If
I but had the strength I would bring the walls crashing
down upon them.

C: Do you want to explore the after life period?
Z: No, not now. I'm being drawn to another lifetime
which is somehow connected to this one.
C: Go to that lifetime.
Z: I see a small, shaggy tan horse. I want more than any-
thing to ride it, but I cannot look forward to any
such thing. I want to play and run and be free.
C: Where are you?
Z: Tibet.
C: Tell me about yourself. Why can't you ride the horse?
Z: I'm a little boy of 7. My father does not want me. He
is afraid of me. I can ride the horse in my mind. I can
feel the wind and ride so fast. It's grand. But I must
not tell. He beats me when I tell of things I do and

calls me liar and is afraid. He takes me far from home.

C: Where is he taking you?

Z: I don't want to look at the place — it's big and dark and frightening. I sense little that is good there. It is a temple, but not like the other temples in our land. Here none searches for enlightenment. They care only for full bellies and the venting of their angers. He takes me to the door and pushes me inside. "Here, he is yours. Do with him what you will. I do not want him."

C: What happened then?

Z: The next eight years were brutal years. I forgot that I could ride the little horse in my mind. I was hungry and cold and beaten often. I worked as a drudge in the kitchen. Sometimes I was allowed to sit in class with boys who were sent there to learn. I learned a little, but not much. The teacher taught with a rod. He often said, "The harder you beat them, the quicker they learn." The days blurred into one another. I lost the awareness of myself. I knew only fear, pain and hunger — and the cold. Even in the summertime when the sun was warm and the mountains green, it was cold within these walls.

C: What happened at the end of the eight years?

Z: Kindness was shown me, the recognition that I am a human being.

C: Who showed you this kindness?

Z: An old and honored teacher on a pilgrimage stopped to stay the night within our walls. I came upon him in a corridor and he placed his hand on my shoulder and looked into my eyes. It was the first time in all those years that anyone had looked at me and seen me as a human being. There was warmth and kindness and wisdom in his face. "Who are you?" he asked me. "I am nothing. I have no name except Boy." "You are a human being," he replied. "You need no name

to be you. Search your heart and mind and you will
remember who and what you are. Learn to heal yourself and then you can heal those around you."

C: What did you do?

Z: I learned to shut out the darkness around me by filling
my mind with the words of the honored teacher. I
remembered the look on his face, the recognition of
me as a person rather than an object to be kicked and
ordered about. I looked within myself and saw that
I despised those around me as they despised me. I was
no better off than they were. I took upon myself a
purpose. I would learn to heal myself.

C: How did you go about this?

Z: The only way I could think of. First I sought out the
ancient books of healing, physical healing. The books
which told which plants and herbs to gather and how
to prepare them for use in healing. I had to start somewhere to fill my mind with good to drive out the
spiteful feelings.

C: What did the others think about this? Did they let
you study?

Z: It was strange. When I no longer acted subservient,
and went purposefully my own way, they left me
alone. I took my rightful share of food and no one
forbade me. I even took extra food and gave to the
other drudges who were hungry.

C: Were they grateful?

Z: No. They simply stuffed their bellies. I could not reach
them as I had been reached by the honored teacher.

C: What followed your studies of healing?

Z: I began to search the mountains and valleys for the
plants and herbs. It was then that my own healing
began. I stood upon the mountan heights and felt
that I stood at the top of the world. I knew that I
wanted to know the One who had created the high

mountains and the whiteness which crowned their peaks, and the golden poppies in the valleys, and all that was here in the world. I learned to look back through the tunnel of time in my mind and found the little boy who could ride the little horse with his mind.

It took me twenty years to heal myself and know that every man is me and I am every man. I learned to treat the ills of body, mind and soul. I gather the plants and special rocks and blend them into that which heals the body. I gather all the joys I have known, and the kindness, and blend them to heal the mind. I gather peace from things which have no time that I know of, to heal the soul.

C: How has this affected those around you?

Z: The poor people in the villages and on the mountains are grateful though they understand nothing more than their freedom from pain. Most of those in the temple despise me and consider gentleness and kindness a sign of weakness. They have named me the "Gatherer of Herbs". A name no longer matters. I need none to know who I am. I have tried to discuss the things I have learned with those who should be able to understand. A few have seen a tiny gleam of light. Most only look at me in cold silence. Their souls are sick beyond my skill to heal. I will love them and treat them with kindness, as I have learned to love myself and, thus, He who created me and them. I will ease their pain with my mind and potions, and perhaps some day they will remember and understand.

C: How did you live out the days of this life?

Z: In my 37th year, I climbed a steep and jagged mountain peak in search of a healing stone. There was a brother from the temple who followed me. I knew he was there but I gave no sign. I knew what was within his heart and that nothing would change the path he had chosen — if it was not now, it would be another time and place. I knew that the most glorious moment of my life was before me if I could make it so.

As he pushed me from the edge, I made myself relax and let love and understanding flow from me to him. I made myself feel as if I floated within the hand of God. It happened quickly, but my mind thought so fast that it seemed like forever. I made myself feel keenly, made myself as aware of sensation as I could possibly be, so that when I hit the slope of jagged rocks below I was aware of every measure of pain. I refused to use that which my mind knew to ease the pain. I felt and cherished every moment, sending love to the one who had been the instrument of my death and all of those who lived within the temple. I thanked God for having been allowed to live this life and come to this moment. I knew in the triumph of that moment that never in those lifetimes to come would any man be able to do to my physical body that which would cloud my mind and take from me my peace, and my desire to love and show gentleness. No man can ever cause me to regret my existence, or hate, or deny my Creator. Only I can allow those things to happen, and with the best that is within me, I will not.

At the moment of death, I was surrounded by the warm light of love and peace. I was free.

And so, Z was able to understand the confused feelings about the use of psychic abilities and remember and renew an important lesson learned long ago.

And now, one last regression to illustrate the broad scope of information available, and especially for those who are fascinated by the romantic legends of Atlantis. These are three different regressions done on three different people spaced several months apart. The first regression was of a man, A, who regressed to a lifetime as the father of the second person, B. B is a female who lived a lifetime as a male, the son of A, and the lover of C. C is a male who lived that lifetime as a female. In the interest of continuity and brevity, most of the questions of the individuals directing the regressions, and much of the repetitive information will be omitted.

A: I am about 20 years old. I am on my way to the temple school to meet my father and two of the elders. They are meeting with me to give me further training in the development and use of my mind. I am of the purple rank, soon to face initiation into the gold. These are designations given because of the color of the robes we wear. Each color indicates the level of knowledge and demonstrated proficiency reached by the initiate. White is the highest rank.

  I enter the room where they are waiting for me. Everything in the room is white and gold and highly polished. There is a design on the floor, a large sun with rays extending around the perimeter. In the center of the sun is a six-pointed star and in the center of the star is a sunken triangle. I sit within the triangle, the three men sit at the three points. They telepathically communicate information to me. Much of it has to do with the humane way to rule. A feeling of strength and power comes with it. This training has been going on for many years. In time, these three will fade into the background and I will become the religious leader of the people. For now, most of the people are at peace and content and in harmony with the Universe. It will not always be so.

(Move ahead several years until you have been ruling for awhile. Look at the political climate and your scope of information. How do you feel about being in charge?)

The three men who taught me have faded into the background. They are using their abilities to seek out and send information to remote and isolated areas of the world where there are people capable of receiving and using the information, though they don't always realize where it comes from.

The weight of the responsibility, knowing that the whole country is looking to me for guidance, trying to stay in harmony with where they are — all the training in the world couldn't prepare me for this. The real guidance and power comes from the center of the Universe.

I am soon to marry. There is a very special woman who has been brought here from the large land mass to the north. She is said to be a direct descendant of the last survivors of our Motherland of Lemuria. I know that the association will be happy and fulfilling. We are in harmony. I'm looking forward to it, but it is not the thing which rules my life. The center of the Universe is my love, my strength, my guidance, and everything else is secondary — such a feeling of completeness.

There is still peace and harmony across the land but not to the degree of when I was 17 or 18. I'm 30 now. Yes, I am of the white rank.

Certain black clouds are gathering around the perimeters of the land. No matter what we do, they don't seem to lessen or go away.

(The time: years later. The person: a female remembering life as A's son.)

B: I'm in a building which has a domed ceiling, like a museum or exhibition hall. It is not a place of worship. It is very ornate, beautiful and colorful. The dome is done in panels and each panel has a gilt border. Around the room are beautiful life-sized alabaster statues of

men and women. The main attraction in the center of
the room is a figure of a female, 25 to 30 ft. tall. Her
arms are reaching out and they are fitted with feathered
wings. I know it is symbolic, not exactly of the soul,
but of the freedom man can have. It's hard to explain.
I'm only a five year old boy. I just know that I like it.
It makes me feel good. This is a profound place.

The woman with me is my mother. She isn't exactly
a priest. She lives at the temple but she is not of the
orders of the temple. She occupies a special position.

Yes, I'm thirteen now. I have on a red shirt which
comes to mid-thigh. Yes, I'm in the second level of
initiation. There is a girl in the first level. She's my
best friend. More than a friend really. I love her. We
will marry when we are old enough. But I'm not
supposed to think about that now.

My mother? She comes from another continent,
the large land mass north of us. Yes, she is racially
different. She has a much fairer skin, dark hair and
eyes. She didn't have to rise through the priesthood
ranks. She had achieved high levels of growth due to
her upbringing. She was accepted by merit as equal
to the highest rank. The story is told that she is a
direct descendant of a last survivor of Lemuria.

(Time: a few years later. Person: A, male, remembering a
life as B's female lover during the last days of Atlantis.)

C: I'm female, very female! About 16. I have long blonde
hair, coppery skin and amber eyes. I am standing
nude on a pedestal. Other girls come in, and in a very
business-like way, start to dress me. There is a sheer
white undergarment and then a robe of bright, bright
royal blue. It's for a religious ceremony, an initiation.
It's very important. Only twelve of us are going to
advance this time. Fewer each time.

The city is large, the buildings like golden glass

with an area in the center of the city similar to Central
Park. There is one large stone building. It looks almost
like an ancient lamasery. I have lived there since I was
eight. I have little memory of the time before. My
parents were priests but we didn't live together as a
family. When I was young I had access to them whenever I wanted, but not a normal parent-child relationship. No, I don't have any negative feelings about it.
I have a brother and a sister who live in the same place.
(What happened after you were dressed for the ceremony?)

After I was dressed I was led to a large room in the
ancient stone building. This is a building which dates
back to the early days of our kingdom. The ceiling is
low, supported by thick pillars. There are many priests
dressed in six different colors denoting different ranks
and functions: white, gold, purple, blue, red and
green. The room is fashioned like a wagon wheel. The
spokes are the aisles leading to the center. As the
twelve of us are led to the center, we form a semi-
circle. The ritual of initiation is conducted by the
white robed priests. We assume a kneeling position
and as the priests touch our heads, the room becomes
very quiet. I am consciously taken out of my body
and led through rites on that level. The blue level
deals with teaching on the astral plane. It is a very big
day in my life. My name? Ta-san-dra — as close as I
can say it in English.

(Note: B is conducting the regression of C.)

I have a lover. As soon as I return to my body I
want to share this with him. My lover is you. You're
male in this lifetime. We are of one mind and body.
They know about us. It's almost as if there is an
unspoken agreement that nothing will be said as long
as we are discreet. Because of the circumstances we
have decided not to take marriage vows yet. Most of

our time together is spent in learning and discovery. You are a little older than me. Not too much. You're being initiated into the gold soon. We're full of life and each other and what we are doing. I don't know much beyond that right now.

The people and the culture? Our city, Cumara, is large and modern in many ways, and yet there are contradictions in various situations. There are mass transit and communication systems, but many of the ways of the people seem archaic. The clothing for example: some is modernistic and skimpy. Some of the women wear jumpsuits with exposed breasts, other mid-thigh or ankle-length robes. Some of the men wear only small crotch pants, others wear everything in between down to long, flowing robes. There are both young and old dressed in every way. Some look almost space-age in their dress, others look like sheepherders on their first visit to town. There doesn't seem to be any particular ethnic or sociological differences, it's the religion. One group is more liberal, another more puritanical.

The time period? The end of the second epoch. The last large island-continent is divided into three parts by large riffs. Atlantis as one continent with outlying islands is ancient history. The destruction is far in the past. It isn't relevant except for the priesthood. A large part of our early schooling dealt with the history of Atlantis back to its colonization by the Motherland of Lemuria.

Cumara is a resort city on the bank of a large river which empties into the sea. It is almost a New Orleans type city. We have traded with the rest of the world in the recent past, but not now. The more modernistic people are either military forces or aligned with the military. Somehow this has to do with the reason why the government closed the ports.

In several quays along the river are the pleasure ships, the swan ships of red, green, gold and blues of the sky and ocean. The priesthood has its own ships. Most are white, but one or two are gold.

In my memory I have just walked into a large boat house. As I walked toward one of the ships, it almost seemed that the swan head turned to look at me with one eye — that feeling, that first fleeting feeling. It's hard not to think of it as alive.

(Go to the age of 30.)

Bad times are upon the land. War is imminent. Our land is doomed. We cannot defend ourselves against the military and they don't fully comprehend the forces they are unleashing. It is a foregone conclusion that we cannot win.

You and I have continued to grow closer, but still have never taken the final marriage vows. There was a private ceremony during which we were inducted into the ranks of the White. We are deeply in love with each other, deeply tied to each other. We are as one. The things they have told us that we must do are devastating to us. Our land will be destroyed. The priesthood will be divided. Some will go. Some will stay. We find it incredible that we must be separated. On other levels we understand and accept because we are dedicated to carrying out the will of Him who made us.

I must go and play a part in establishing a new beginning for evolving man somewhere else on this planet. The decision has been made to discard the traditions and ways of the centuries and chart a new, simpler spiritual path for man to walk. Those who cannot play a vital role in that will remain here to help until the end. You will stay to guide them through that time.

There is one swan ship where we used to meet to be together. I am to take that ship and two others and leave with a small band for another land. You and I share our parting time aboard that ship as we have shared so many days and nights. We are both certain that your death is imminent — a few days, or weeks at most. I, too, face the possibility of death, going to primitive lands, virtually among savages, in order that the truths we know will not be lost to the world. I feel inadequate but I must go.

I remember standing on the deck of the ship looking back at the city, watching it grow smaller. Then the swan ship spreads its wings and takes flight so that we ride just above the surface of the waves. We speed along for several days and then the ship settles into the water off a fog-shrouded coast. I can see the waves breaking on the shore, but I cannot see inland.

The next day, I am still aboard the ship when I am stunned by a heavy blow. You are dead, and all the others are dead — all gone. Your spirit has fled to me. You are filled with the horror of what you have witnessed and such profound sadness. I sit quietly for many hours and commune with you until you are at peace. Then it is time for me and the others to disembark and make a new beginning.

Chapter Five

Some Case Histories

Through the years of working with regressions, both directing regressions and being regressed, there are few situations which occur in life that haven't surfaced. The following cases are examples of various problems and situations and how the regression experience helped in understanding and dealing with them. These are meant only as guides to help you learn to look for and recognize significant patterns and events. What causes a trauma in one person may leave another unmarred, so keep an open mind when looking for the cause of a problem. It may not be what you expect, and if you spend your time looking for something to fit a preconceived idea, you may miss the real cause.

Fears and Phobias

One of the most common problems man faces is fear, and often these fears become phobias. I define a phobia as a *seemingly* irrational and persistent fear which is socially paralyzing. Reactions which are abnormal and out of proportion to the threat (if any) presented are consistently triggered by the same object, event, environment, or person.

Fire

Many years ago I was conversing with a young woman in my home and casually lit a cigarette. She recoiled in horror and shakily admitted that she lived in fear of fire — any kind of fire. If someone lit a candle or match in her presence, she felt unreasonable panic, began to tremble and perspire and usually ran from the room in tears. This was most embarrassing and uncomfortable to her and she recognized that the response was not appropriate to the situation and completely out of control. Neither she nor her parents could think of any childhood trauma which could account for her fear.

During the course of a regression, we discovered that, in her most recent past life, she had been trapped on the top floor of an old frame farm house and had burned to death. Using the positive closing statements of the regression technique released most of the trauma involved. Afterward we discussed the fact that those circumstances were unlikely to recur in this lifetime and she had no need to react to fire in that way. She said that just knowing what had caused the phobia lifted a tremendous burden from her mind and she felt a freedom that she couldn't remember having ever felt. She requested a book of matches. I was a little hesitant but got them for her. She took a deep breath and struck one. As she held the burning match, the most beautiful smile of relief crossed her face. One by one she burned every match in the book without the slightest reaction.

This was a rather dramatic recovery from a very severe phobia. Not all fears are so instantaneously resolved.

Snakes

I have known several people who were morbidly afraid of snakes, poisonous and nonpoisonous. Most people have, at least, a healthy respect for them though the danger is somewhat overrated. In the U.S. you run a greater risk of being struck by lightning than dying of a snakebite.

Early on, having one daughter who has an affinity for anything that creeps or crawls, I learned to be comfortable in the presence of snakes and all sorts of odd creatures. And a little knowledge and common sense has helped me avoid any problems on my many wilderness outings. So, snakes were the last thing on my mind as I was preparing to take some new friends into the wilderness. We were in a store buying some last minute items and I wasn't paying much attention to the others when the young son of one of the men ran up and stuck something in his father's hand and said, "Daddy, will you need one of these?" I heard a choking sound and turned around to see the daddy in question shaking, ashen, staring in terror at his hand, and gasping for breath. It took a minute for me to realize what the problem was. The young son had handed his father a snakebite kit on which was pictured the head of a snake with open mouth and prominent fangs.

I grabbed the kit and led him away from the area, talking in a soothing manner. The trauma began to subside and we went outside and sat in the car. He told me that he could't remember having ever been around a live snake but that he always reacted like this when he saw a snake on television or in a movie or book or magazine. Right away I knew we had more of a problem than he realized. There were many harmless water snakes and a few rattlers in the area where we planned to camp. If a picture could have the effect I had witnessed, I could only imagine what coming face to face with a live snake might provoke.

We intended to leave early the following morning, so

I explained the problem to him and asked if he was willing to do a regression that evening. He agreed. He regressed to a lifetime in India where he had been bitten by a krait, a snake akin to a cobra, and he had died a painful and traumatic death.

After the regression we discussed the particular types of snakes in the area where we were going and their bites and how they differed from a krait. I outlined normal precautions which would make an encounter with a rattlesnake unlikely and assured him that I always carried an antivenom kit. We also discussed the fact that few snakebites result in death. He cautiously looked at a picture of a snake and had little reaction.

I felt that we had had reasonable success when, a few days later, he stood several feet from a cute little grass snake and only shuddered slightly and said, "What an ugly, slimy creature." Then he looked at me and grinned, "Well, at least they don't throw me into a panic any more, but don't expect me to love the little beggars."

We knew another individual, a young woman, who exhibited unusual courage and determination every day as she often literally battled for her physical survival in a ghetto high school, determined to teach the students to read. I don't think I could have faced the daily threat of physical assault, or having furniture broken over my head, or having to carry an axe handle to protect myself in the halls and parking lot as she did. She appeared fearless and very much in control of herself until faced with a snake or anything resembling a snake. This could immediately reduce her to a trembling, ashen bundle of tears and hysteria.

During a regression, she remembered a lifetime when, as a very young child, she lived in a crude hut on a swampy island. She was cornered in the hut by a large, poisonous snake and bitten repeatedly. She died alone, a very painful and frightening death. Re-living this episode was a very emotional experience for her, but the relief she derived from it was immense and her fear of snakes assumed a normal level of healthy respect.

And then, there is the case of one of my soul friends who isn't really afraid of anything except snakes. He has eagerly regressed back into all kinds of situations except any dealing with that particular fear. His reason: "I don't want to not be afraid of snakes." And, of course, that piques my curiosity mightily.

Fear of Doctors

I had occasion to work with a young woman who expressed an inordinate fear of doctors and any laboratory or hospital type of environment. This had caused her many problems and repeated embarrassingly traumatic episodes. The memories of having been forced to have the required innoculations before beginning school were terrifying. She had turned down several excellent job opportunities which required a physical. Though she was very much in love with a young man, even the thought of the required blood test had made her hesitant to accept his marriage proposal. There, too, was the prospect of having babies to be considered.

She had not discussed any of this with me at the time of her first regression. During the regression, after having scanned one lifetime, her initial impression of the second was of a cattle car and barbed wire. She immediately expressed a desire to terminate the session without explanation. A few days later, during a second session she again approached that lifetime and brushed it aside saying she had died at a young age and went on to another lifetime. Afterward I asked her about the incident and she replied that there was something dreadful in that lifetime that she didn't want to let herself remember. Then she suddenly began talking about her fear of doctors and hospitals. I explained to her that the fear might have its roots in the lifetime she was avoiding and that if she could let herself remember and understand, she would probably find the fear much easier to deal with and not nearly so much of a handicap. She thought about it for a few days and came back saying that she wanted to remember, because after all it was only a memory.

I approached this regression with a great deal of care, using frequent repetitions of the phrases meant to help her remain detached from the situation. What emerged was the most disgusting, horrifying, angering story I have ever heard. Listening to her voice, I could almost see the events as they unfolded. She had been a young Jewish girl, just at puberty, during WW II. She had been taken from her family, confined in a concentration camp, and separated out for medical experimentation. She had been most obscenely, inhumanly used, abused, mutilated, and put on display and ridiculed. It would have been a horrible experience for anyone, but for a sensitive, emotionally vulnerable child already trying to deal with the normally confusing emotions of puberty and the trauma of separation from home and family, it was totally devastating. Death was welcomed.

This young woman released a great deal of the trauma of that lifetime during the regression and emerged with a healthy anger toward the people who had done this to her, and determined that they would not ruin a second lifetime for her. At last contact, she was married and happily anticipating the birth of her first child.

MISCELLANEOUS CASES

An Alcohol Problem

In my studies I had come across two case histories of alcoholics who had no connection with each other, had lived in different countries, and had been treated by two different hypnotherapists several years apart. The fact that made these cases stick in my mind was that both had been regressed into a past life, one deliberately and the other by accident, and both had hit on almost identical reasons for the problems with alcohol. I had regressed several alcoholics, not with that problem in mind, and had never run into a similar episode. A few years later, I was intrigued to hear a familiar pattern emerging during the regression of a man whom I had only recently met. He re-lived a lifetime in which he was a Confederate soldier, very young and very frightened. He just wanted to be away from the blood and noise and battle and blot it all from his mind. During the latter days of the Civil War, he was seriously wounded. There was no medical help to be had, but one of his buddies had part of a bottle of whiskey. There was only enough to dull the pain for a little while. The young man died a couple of days later with a raging desire for more alcohol to make the pain go away and blot out all the horror around him.

After the regression the man began to cry and told me that he couldn't remember a time in his life when he hadn't wanted a drink. He had tried various types of treatment and had been involved with several groups, but each time the help was temporary. Now he felt that he had some solid information that he could work with. We did some other regressions and discovered another lifetime prior to the Civil War period during which he had developed a habit of heavy drinking when he wanted to avoid dealing with problems. (Often deep-seated problems or fears will have roots in more than one lifetime.) Having determined that these two lifetimes were the only ones in which alcohol played a significant role, I rephrased the positive statements at the end of the last regression saying, "You will bring with you the beneficial knowledge and understanding on all levels of why you have the strong desire to drink alcoholic beverages. You will leave behind, on all levels, the detrimental need and desire to drink alcoholic beverages.

I didn't hear from him for several months, then he called me and told me of his progress. His desire to drink had been almost nonexistent, but when the desire had been triggered during the first few weeks, he would tell himself that now that he understood what had caused the problem, the reason to drink no longer existed. He said that the desire was easily controlled and then ceased to be there. He went on to say that occasionally he found himself in a social or business situation where it was very awkward to turn down a drink. He said that he could now take one drink and nurse it through the evening and never have the desire for another. Over a period of years while we were still in contact, this continued to be the situation.

This, of course, is not the answer to every alcohol or drug problem, but for those who are seeking help, it is worth exploring. There is always the possibility that information will be found which will aid in more conventional treatment of these problems.

An Unusual Compulsion

Many years ago we met a man who was subject to an unusual bit of compulsive behavior. He bought coats. This man had closets full of coats and it was unusual to see him at any time of the year without a jacket on or close at hand. Scarcely a month passed when he wasn't showing off a new purchase, and sometimes more frequently. He could go into a store with a specific purchase in mind but if he spied a rack of coats, that was where he ended up. Now, in some of the northern climes this might not appear bizarre, but he lived in an area of Texas where a light jacket is adequate for all but a few of the coldest winter days.

Most of his travels took him south to Mexico or Central America — the warmer the better. The only times I knew him to venture past the Red River were during the summer months when he would go outfitted like 'Nanook of the North'. My husband and I were quite puzzled over this behavior from a man who had a very logical, analytical mind and seemed little interested in amassing any great amount of personal possessions. Faced with the choice of spending his last dollar on food or a coat, the coat won out every time.

It all became quite clear during a regression when he re-lived a life spent outdoors in the far north where he was cold most of his life. Finding himself in a desperate situation where death from freezing was imminent, he promised himself that if he survived he would never be cold again. He died with that thought in mind and has spent this life trying to keep that promise to himself. Now his coat wardrobe is somewhat smaller and he is much more likely to come out of a store with what he went in for, but he still likes to have several good warm coats on hand 'just in case'.

Necktie Party

There were two people of our acquaintance, a man and a woman, who had similar aversions to wearing anything snug around their necks. No blouses or shirts buttoned all the way up, no turtlenecked sweaters, no scarves, and for the man the necessity of wearing a necktie was like being asked to face a firing squad. Anything which caused the least pressure around their necks produced choking sensations and feelings of nausea. In both cases, regressions revealed lifetimes in which they had died by hanging.

I don't know what the long-term result of the regression was for the man. I can only speak for the woman. I still don't wear turtlenecked sweaters but I have learned to be comfortable with a bandana loosely knotted around my neck during my wilderness treks.

"Damn that Horse"

Having grown up around horses and ridden every chance I got as a child, it never entered my mind that I would marry a man who hated horses. It was too late when I found out. We'd been married fifteen years. Up until then we had lived in the city and the question hadn't arisen. Then we moved to a rural area. I was delighted when the people who owned the property next to us and the family who moved in across the road acquired some horses. I watched with a great deal of pride and amusement, and just a twinge of fear, when our fearless five year old would sneak across the road and entice the horses to the fence with some tidbit. Then she would climb the fence, balance on the fence post, and jump astride her favorite steed and ride around the pasture without even a bridle until the horse would return to the fence and she would reverse the procedure.

I didn't let her know that I knew — why spoil half the fun? But I encouraged both girls to make friends with the horse which lived next door to us. Every afternoon we could look across our driveway and see him stretching across the fence waiting for us to come out and pet him and feed him choice clumps of grass. We were doing this one evening when my husband came home from work. I called him to join us. His reaction took me by surprise. He didn't want to have any contact with the horse, nor did he want us to. I told him what our youngest had been doing in an effort to show him how gentle the horses were. His reply: "Horses are mean, unpredictable and untrustworthy. Just stay away from them. All horses should be shot!"

I couldn't believe what I was hearing. This was the man who had hand-fed a baby bird blown out of a nest until it could fly. This was the man who brought home stray kittens and puppies, a newborn jack rabbit taken from a dog's mouth, and even an orphaned baby skunk.

This was the man who had turned our acre into a menagerie. And he hated horses!

I asked him if he had had some bad experience as a child with a horse. He said that he hadn't, that, "I hate horses and horses hate me."

It was a good while later that the reason surfaced. During a regression one evening he remembered a lifetime in which he was being pursued by a group of men on horseback. He was about to elude them when his horse stumbled and threw him and then ran off and left him. The men caught him and hung him on the spot for something he didn't do. He died hating and cursing that horse.

It has taken him awhile of thinking about it, but just the other day he asked me if there was anywhere around where we could rent some horses. He wants to learn how to ride.

One for Women's Lib

You might not always find the cause for an attitude in a past life, but sometimes a cure is there anyway. We have a dear and delightful friend who has a very macho air and appearance. When we first met, usually his manners toward women were strictly 'southern gentlemen'. But on occasion he would express an attitude about women in general which would make me want to plant my foot firmly on the seat of his pants.

One day we were doing regressions just for grins, and he said he didn't have anything specific in mind, that I could choose any direction I wanted. I knew my time had come. I directed him to go back to any lifetime he had lived as a female, preferably a wife and mother. We hit a goldmine!

He was a very intelligent, well-educated young woman who found herself in the role of a pioneer wife with a house full of babies. I let him savor the memories of coping with the 'monthlies' under primitive conditions, pregnancy, childbirth, the day to day drudgery of meals and laundry and coping with a cranky, demanding and unappreciative husband, and survival in general on the frontier. He remembered what it felt like to have few, if any rights, and be considered an ignorant, second class citizen because he was a female.

It was quite a revelation to him. I suspect that if he happens to return in his next lifetime as a woman, it will be as an ardent feminist.

Family Friction

There was a teenaged boy from a very close-knit family who was troubled by the ongoing friction between him and his grandfather. They loved each other dearly and missed each other when they were separated, but simply could not get along when they were together. This had been the case practically since birth.

As far back as he could remember, the boy had resented any instruction or personal comment from the grandfather and the fact that his grandfather did not treat him as an adult. The grandfather overreacted to any comment made by the boy, accusing him of trying to run his life and acting like he knew more about everything than his grandfather. The atmosphere when they were together was one of hostility, each waiting for the other to do or say something that would cause offense. Neither one reacted this way with anyone else in any situation.

Past-life regression information revealed that the boy had been his grandfather's father in this lifetime — his own great-grandfather. The great-grandfather had died just a few years before the boy's birth. He had been a very strict and domineering father, constantly criticizing his son and making him feel inadequate and insecure. He had demanded strict obedience and at least a show of respect. Age had not mellowed him.

The son (grandfather) had resented his father all of his life but had loved him and wanted to please him or at least have his approval. There were times when his feelings had almost bordered on hate. On numerous occasions when the son had been embarked on some ventures, his father had stepped in with advice and instruction and caused him to lose confidence in himself and fail.

Small wonder there was friction between these two. The grandson wanted his grandfather to treat him with the same deference he had demanded as his father. The grandfather instinctively recognized the personality of his domineering father in his grandson and reacted accordingly.

The knowledge brought great relief to the situation. Though the grandfather's beliefs precluded his being made aware of this information, the boy's parents understood and accepted it. They were able to help the boy modify his actions toward his grandfather and deal with his grandfather and deal with his own frustrations and resentments. The situation is still not ideal, but the tensions have greatly eased and grandson and grandfather are frequently able to spend a day together without friction.

Suicide

Suicide is a difficult and complex subject. It is impossible to cover every aspect in a work such as this. I don't have all the answers, only perhaps a little insight and experience to offer in the hope that it will provide some help and understanding for someone.

To my mind, suicide is not a subject which can be confined within strict boundaries of right and wrong or black and white. There are an infinite number of shades of grey. Motivations and circumstances have to play a significant role in considering the karmic aspects. There is a vast difference between someone who commits suicide as an act of self-sacrifice to save others from death, betrayal or misery and someone who commits suicide as an escape from emotional pain or problems. Even then, it is a difficult thing to judge unless you have experienced the depths of depression which the human spirit is capable of reaching — that emotional pain which has no counterpart in the physical — where the feeling of being alone is so profound that life seems utterly without purpose and you feel so helpless and hopeless that there seems no place to turn for help, no way that you can even communicate the despair, and there is even the lack of desire to seek help. There is that moment which comes when the pain is so intense that you make a pact with yourself that you are not going to hurt any more and that you won't ever hurt that way again. This brings a feeling of calm and that is the moment when the decision is made to carry out the act of suicide so that the pain won't return. But it is the decision to quit hurting, to do something about it, which brings the calm, not the decision to die. Death holds out a false promise of oblivion with an end to problems. But the problems and the pain are still there after death and in the next lifetime and the next, until you understand that there is nowhere to turn. The only way to escape is to make that decision not to hurt any more and live and accept that no person or circumstance is worth allowing yourself to build that much pain and misery into your life.

If there is someone around you whom you suspect of suicidal feelings, don't be afraid to ask them and to listen. Forget the platitudes. If you haven't been there, you don't know how they feel. Let them know that you love them and you care, and that you will help them in every way you can. Don't hesitate to tell those around them who care about them and can give constructive help. If you can get them interested in regression, so much the better, because it may provide answers that they need and it may be that the cold, hard fact of experiencing survival after death and the law of cause and effect which makes the difference.

For twenty-two years we enjoyed a marvelous friendship with a man I shall call Jim. Jim was exceptionally intelligent, warm, kind, generous and gentle. He spoke several languages fluently, and everything he touched turned to money. He enjoyed living well, but he was one of the most unselfish human beings I have ever known. On the surface it would seem that he had everything, but that wasn't the case.

Jim was an extremely sensitive person and very much a 'Pollyanna'. He always expected everyone to be as kind and honest as he was, and when they weren't, he felt that it was his fault. It was only after years of hurt, bewilderment and betrayal that he began to express a more realistic attitude about people, though I suspect that deep inside he never quite lost his idealistic expectations.

Jim had made the mistake of allowing his sense of self-worth and his self-image to be shaped by what others thought of him — his parents in particular. No matter what he accomplished during his school career or later in his profession — and his achievements were considerable — he never had a word of praise from his parents. If he got 99 on an exam, the response was, "Why wasn't it 100?" If he made 100, there still wasn't any praise. It was just what they expected of him. He allowed their attitude to blind him to his own achievements. But praise wasn't what Jim really wanted. He wanted to be loved and he felt that there must be some flaw within him because his parents didn't seem to care. The problem was that Jim hadn't learned to love himself. In addition to this, Jim had a physical problem which caused him to be grossly overweight.

During his late teens and twenties, Jim was often depressed and suicidal. We talked often and I felt rather helpless because I was young and inexperienced in such matters. Also, Jim did not believe in any type of Supreme Being or that there was anything after death. My religious beliefs at that time held no common meeting ground for us. During his thirties the pattern of hurt and disillusionment intensified and he wanted an end to his misery. He made two serious attempts at suicide, but both times I had sensed what was occurring and had gotten help to him in time. Part of me understood and sympathized, but during this time I had come to a belief in reincarnation and had begun to work with regression. Through this Jim finally came to understand and believe that death didn't mean an end to anything. In his past lives he began to see the reasons for some of his problems and he discovered that a pattern had developed in which he had used suicide in numerous lifetimes in an attempt to escape. He determined to resolve as many of the problems as he could, and learn to live with those he couldn't. He began to like himself a little more and learned to accept that there were those of us who loved and respected him very much. He put forth his best effort under extremely difficult circumstances. During the last few years of his life when it seemed, for want of a better way to express it, that the whole universe dumped on him, he held on and maintained his kind and loving nature.

When he became ill and suspected that he wouldn't recover, he telephoned and talked to us and never gave a hint that everything wasn't fine. We didn't suspect that he was bedfast. Later when he knew that he was dying, he did one last unselfish act which was typical of him. He refused to allow us to be notified because he didn't want to upset our holiday plans that year.

Jim's life was never easy, but he managed to resolve a great many problems which won't face him in future lives and he freed himself from the cycle of suicide.

It was a tiny pueblo village where a soul friend and I lived. We had been born at almost the same moment and had immediately developed a great affinity for each other based on several similar lifetimes. Though I was female and he was male, we refused traditional roles and there was little in our lives that we did not share. It was inevitable that we become husband and wife. We had been wedded only a short while when hostile Indians raided our village and began to kill everyone in sight. He was mortally wounded but I managed to get him to a place of safety and held him as he died. I could not imagine life without him. I gave no thought to the future or that others might need me. I only wanted to follow where he had gone. I took his knife and killed myself.

It is difficult to find words to describe the impact of what followed. It seemed that we were still in our beloved mountains. He was just ahead of me — disappearing just around a bend in the canyon or over a ridge top. I called but he didn't hear. No matter how fast I ran I could never catch up with him. The depth of loneliness and despair are indescribable. There was no way to measure time, but it seemed to go on forever. Then I stopped to think and plan, and when his figure stopped, I saw that I had been pursuing an illusion, and I understood that I had had no right to take my life.

In a later lifetime, the relationship was renewed. There came a time when it was necessary for us to go our own separate ways and the pain and despair was there again. I found myself believing that I could not ever find any joy in life again, and that continuing to live was too painful. I made the decision that the pain would stop. In the calm which followed, instead of taking my life, it occurred to me that nothing was worth that price. I realized that as long as I depended upon someone else to make me a whole person, I would be incomplete and any joy would be fragile and impermanent. So I chose, in that lifetime, to live and turn my energies to living instead of weeping. And I became a whole person and found that I had purpose in life. I gained a lasting joy and a love that was not built on need or dependency. And I didn't hurt again.

Antagonisms Within Friendships

We renewed acquaintance with a friend from lifetimes past. There were many strong ties and he immediately became like a member of the family. We explored many spiritual and psychic highways and byways together. At one time, without hesitation, he jumped into the middle of a situation which could easily have cost his life, to save mine.

In spite of this, there were odd moments when he would withdraw into a shell and exhibit a puzzling antagonism toward me. It didn't extend to other members of our family — just me. When I finally got him to talk to me about it, he said that ever so often he would suddenly feel a deep distrust and anger toward me that he couldn't explain. We agreed to look for the answer to this disturbing situation.

We found the answer in a lifetime where we had been male cousins. My father was a petty chieftain over a handful of desert nomads, and my friend was the son of his favorite brother. We were very close during boyhood, but as we became older, it seemed that he was everything my father desired in a son. I was never quite as good at anything as he was, and though my father praised us both, I was certain that my father favored him. I became more and more jealous and resentful and afraid that he would usurp my place. I was careful to hide my feelings. I bided my time, and one day when we were far away from the others, I overpowered him and bound and gagged him and left him hidden in a gully to die. I couldn't bring myself to kill him outright. Later I came upon his skeleton, and laughed as I scattered his bones.

He had been baffled by my actions. To that moment, he believed us to be the closest of comrades, and he had no understanding of the reason for my cruelty to him.

After we had both explored that lifetime and discussed the emotions generated, we discussed other more positive lifetimes since that time where no antagonisms had been present. It took awhile for us to understand what had caused those old feelings to surface in this lifetime. The answer was in our martial arts class where we were often sparring partners and competed against each other. This had stirred old memories of our boyhood scuffles and competitions in that long ago life. After we understood and released the feelings, his antagonism disappeared and trust was restored.

In another instance, two couples met and became friends. However, after a few months, Betty became very antagonistic toward Nina. There had been no incident, no problems that Nina was aware of. Even direct questioning of Betty brought the puzzling answer that Nina had neither done nor said anything to upset her. Betty felt a growing hatred of Nina and became vindictive and verbally abusive toward her. Nina had no corresponding emotions toward Betty. She did everything she could think of to change the situation with no effect, and finally decided that her only alternative was to avoid Betty. The situation troubled Nina and was never far from her mind.

Sometime later, during a regression, Nina stumbled upon a lifetime in which Betty and Betty's present husband, Charles, had also been husband and wife. Charles had married Betty for her wealth and social position. Charles already possessed vast holdings and was somewhat of a petty dictator in the area where he lived. Betty was a few years older than Charles, and he never let her forget it. They had been married many years, and were well into middle age when Charles became enamored of Nina, a pretty young widow with a son who lived in the nearby village. Charles forced Nina to be his mistress by holding her son hostage. He forced Nina and Betty to live in the same house and take their meals together. He flaunted the relationship and caused Betty a great deal of pain. She blamed Nina and hated her. Nina understood Betty's antagonism and felt only pity for her.

While the regression information helped Nina to understand Betty's animosity, Betty chose not to deal with it and continued to feed her negative feelings. Nina knew that she had done all that she could, and chose to let go of the situation and get on with her life without any guilt feelings.

A Lesbian Understands

A middle-aged woman consulted me about a lesbian relationship in which she had been involved as the dominant partner for many years. Trouble had suddenly surfaced in the relationship, and the woman was feeling mental and emotional confusion and distress over her lesbian orientation.

During a rather lengthy regression the woman found that she had lived her last several lifetimes as a very macho male. In each lifetime she had lived in a cultural situation in which women were relegated to a status of just barely human, and everything strongly masculine was admired and cultivated. In her present lifetime, her father had been a very domineering person who had treated her and her mother as little more than servants, while her brother got every consideration.

She could clearly see how her childhood situation had triggered the carry over of the macho attitudes from the past lives and had caused her to want to reject her own femininity. We could only theorize what had triggered her present dissatisfaction with herself. She expressed the desire to explore her femininity and develop a more balanced attitude. She also expressed the determination to make some friends of the male sex in order to prove to herself that they were not all of a domineering nature. She had avoided contact with men as much as possible out of the fear that she would be dominated and degraded.

As often happens, I had no further contact with her for a few years. One day I was shopping when a very attractive lady approached me. "You don't recognize me, do you?" And I didn't until she told me her name. She said that it had been difficult and frightening, but she had set out to find out about being a woman. She had cultivated a feminine appearance and had started moving in social circles where she could meet and get to know men as well as women. She had realized that her attitude toward women had been as affected as her other attitudes toward life. She found many individuals of both sex whom she could enjoy and respect as human beings. She began to thoroughly enjoy being a woman as she realized that it didn't mean being weak and subservient. She had met, fallen in love with and married a very fine man. She felt very comfortable and happy in her heterosexual relationship.

This is not meant as a comment one way or another on the gay community. This is just the story of what happened to one human being, and why.

Racial Prejudice

I met a very nice older lady, a rather typical WASP raised in the deep South. She was very cultured and genteel, and a bigot with a capital B. She had never allowed herself the opportunity to know any black people, and was quite mystified and distressed at my having several black friends. To her, dark skin was synonymous with ignorance, inferiority, poverty and filth. The vocabulary she used on this subject caused me a great deal of embarrassment and anger.

I had known her a good while when she expressed the

desire to be regressed. She revisited a rather mundane life-time and then I directed her into another. When I told her to look down at her feet, the strangest expression crossed her face. Her voice got fainter and fainter as she described her appearance in that lifetime. She was a member of a small primitive tribe in Africa, and very black. After the first shock of her skin color wore off, she became very involved in the joys and sorrows and events of that lifetime. She was very quiet when we finished the regression and didn't show much inclination to discuss it. I didn't press her because I knew she had a great deal to think about.

As the weeks passed, she never mentioned the regression, but I noted that certain derogatory terms had been dropped from her vocabulary. I had to make a short business trip and asked her to accompany me. She was quite eager to go since one of the people I was going to see was somewhat of a celebrity. What neither of us knew was that another friend would be present at the meeting, and that friend would embody everything she had expressed fear and disgust of in the past. He was tall and muscular and very talented, but my gentle, fierce-looking friend had very, very black skin and classic Negroid features.

After introductions, she was left alone with him in an adjoining room while I took care of business. I was somewhat relieved and amused to catch glimpses of them sitting on a small couch in animated conversation. Later, on the way home, she exclaimed, "He was one of the nicest and most interesting people I've ever met." I just looked at her and grinned. She turned a deep red. "I did learn something from that regression, and even more today," she said. "People are people — individuals — and you can't make blanket judgements on the basis of race."

The Other Side of the Coin
I was teaching a series of mind development classes

out of town to quite a mixed group of humanity. In the class was a young black man who was well-educated and widely traveled. He was quite interested in what I was teaching, but it was obvious that he was carrying a rather large chip on his shoulder. He didn't make a great deal of effort to conceal his contempt for anyone whose skin was lighter than his, and he was determined to make everyone very aware of his 'blackness'. During one of the breaks he stood on the fringes of a small group which had gathered around to ask me some questions about reincarnation. He asked a question or two. Later he asked if he could make arrangements to be regressed. Since he was leaving the country a few days later, I agreed to regress him that evening after the class.

"Oh my god!" he said as we began the regression "I'm white!" Disgust and disbelief was evident in his tone. "My skin is white," he repeated with a shudder. Not only was he white, he was an overseer on a plantation in Alabama prior to the Civil War and treated the slaves none too kindly. We went from that lifetime to one in China, and then to another in which he was not only white, he was female.

When I directed him back to the present, he sat up and began to cry with deep, wracking sobs. I knew that what was happening to him was a very healing thing. Shortly he was smiling through his tears. "I guess I really earned the chance to see things from a dark perspective, didn't I? You know, I've always thought of myself as black, but now I realize that I'm not black, I'm me. I just happen to be inhabiting a black, male body this time." He stopped and thought for a moment. "Hey, that means that the world is populated by 'mes' that just happen to be living in different kinds of bodies, but the me-essence isn't black or white or red or male or female — it just is. Say, lady, how come you chose the body of a 'honky broad' this time?" he ended with a chuckle.

He was right. Our awareness, our self, is neither male or female, black or white or any other color. It simply is, and the particular bodies we inhabit are our costumes for the roles we play during our appearances on the stage of the planet Earth.

The Fear of Death

I was asked by a couple of doctors to work with a patient of theirs. He was terminally ill with cancer. He was still able to be out of the hospital and relatively free from pain, but the man as well as the doctors knew that he had some bad days ahead. They wanted me to teach him some pain control and self-hypnosis techniques to make things easier for him. They also hoped that through teaching him mental control of some of his body processes, the progress of the disease might be slowed.

Outwardly the man did not appear to be all that ill, but the doctors had told me privately that everything that could be done for him had been done, and within a few months, if he survived that long, things were going to get pretty rough. The man was very cooperative, and mastered the pain control and self-hypnosis techniques quickly. It was evident, however, that he wanted something more from me, but was hesitant to ask.

I hoped that my intuition was right. I took a deep breath and plunged in. "Would you like to talk about dying?" I asked.

"Yes, yes I would," he said with a great sigh of relief. "People don't want to talk about dying to someone who is. Everyone avoids the subject and gets uncomfortable if I bring it up. All they do is assure me that I'll get better when we all know I won't. I need to talk about it. I need to make peace with the idea. I'm afraid to die. I'm angry about dying. I don't know what will happen to me. Maybe no one does, but I need to be able to talk about being afraid."

He talked for a long time and we discussed many things. When it seemed appropriate, I brought up the subject of reincarnation. He said that he knew very little about the subject, but would be open-minded even though he felt that it would probably be in conflict with his religious beliefs.

I briefly outlined the theory and he found that there wasn't as much conflict as he had supposed. He expressed a desire to experience regression though he wasn't sure that he could believe in reincarnation. I regressed him through several lifetimes, paying special attention to taking him through his death experiences in detail and allowing him to explore the in-between-life periods thoroughly.

He was very peaceful and thoughtful when we finished. "I can't explain how I know," he said, "but I know that those were true memories of things I have experienced. It explains so much to me about my present life and relationships. And I'm not afraid of dying anymore. It's nothing. I've done it so many times I ought to be pretty good at it by now. I just wish that I could communicate some of this to my family and friends, but they are very skeptical even about the pain control and self-hypnosis. They would think that I was grasping at straws. I don't want to spend the time I have left in theological discussions. It's enough that I know."

He lived comfortably a lot longer than anyone expected and died a peaceful death in his own bed.

These case histories should give you some idea of the versatility and usefulness of regression. While these examples show instances of problems understood and solved, you must remember that each person is different and his or her scope of information and experience is different Also, regressing and understanding the source of a problem is not enough. The person or persons involved must be

willing to accept their personal responsibilities in the situations, and be willling to let go of the emotions. If all that
you gain from a regression experience which reveals the
source of a problem is a feeling of guilt, or you and the
persons involved use the experience as a basis for trying to
assign guilt to each other, then the experience has been
misused and has become a detrimental experience for all
concerned. The purpose of regression is understanding,
freedom, forgiving and forgetting, and moving on to a
more productive life.

Recurring Positive and Negative Patterns

One of the most important reasons for keeping easily
accessible records to your regressions is to be able to detect
recurring positive or negative patterns of behavior. Many
times a person is not consciously aware of behavior patterns
which work well and should be positively reinforced.

In scanning past-life information, first pay attention
tc your patterns of success and failure. The particular situations in which you were successful are less important than
the actions and attitudes which led to the successes. Study
the types of people you interacted with and how you dealt
with them, your feelings about yourself, your feelings
about your prospects for success, the efforts you were
willing to put into succeeding, and the efforts which success
had on you and your life. This last is very important. Then
study your failures. Try to determine why you failed. Did
you learn from the failures, or did you allow them to be
defeats which kept you from trying again? What were your
feelings about yourself in regard to failure? Did you allow
either failure or success to change your self-image? Pay
attention to your emotional reactions. What triggered
them? Did you feel threatened or intimidated by particular types of people or situations? Do these same patterns,
positive or negative, continue to repeat in this lifetime?

As you study this information, do you find patterns of self-defeating actions? Are there times when you put everything into a situation which was necessary to insure success, and then just before the culmination of your efforts did you just quit or make some decision which turned the situation from success to failure?

This is more common than you might suppose, both in past lives and present lives. This is why it is important to examine what effects past successes had on you and your lives. You may find one or more instances in which success seemed to bring a great deal of added responsibility which you did not want, or it changed relationships with people you cared about, or you allowed it to change you in a way that you did not like, or life became dull and unchallenging because you did not establish additional goals. If you were not able to deal well with these situations, you may have begun a pattern of being afraid or reluctant to succeed. I have repeatedly observed individuals putting years of effort into reaching a goal, only to appear to deliberately make decisions at the last moment to insure failure. If you can objectively look at past and present lives and see this type of pattern and accept responsibility for it, then you can change it.

Make an effort to find and understand the lifetimes in which any of the foregoing behavior patterns originated. The positive statements at the end of the regression technique will go a long way in helping you to get the negative influences out of your life and reinforce the positive. Understanding the origin is another valuable tool. Then determine the changes you want to make in your behavior patterns. Imagine yourself in various scenarios which are appropriate to the circumstances, and rehearse the role of yourself fully in control, acting in a positive, confident, successful manner. Whenever you find that you are replaying mental scenes with yourself cast in a negative role, make the conscious effort to replay that scenario and change your actions to a positive role. Then, when such situations occur in real life, make a conscious, deliberate effort to play the positive role which you have created in your mind. You control the situation instead of allowing the situation to control you.

Create in your mind the image of the person you want to be. Look on it as if it is a role which you are creating for a play. Think about the people you deal with who make you feel awkward or intimidated in some way. Imagine yourself feeling confident and at ease in their presence. Then, when such situations do occur, slip into the role which you have created in your mind. It may be a little difficult at first to stay in the role, but the more you do it, the more it will become natural to you. Others will begin reacting to the new you, and treating you in a more positive manner.

Just remember that failure is not a defeat if you use it as a steppingstone to success. Success is not always a triumph if it doesn't bring you what you really want.

Age Regression

By this time you may think that the solutions to most of your problems in this lifetime are to be found in past lifetimes. Actually, a great many of the problems which we deal with on a day to day basis have origins in the early years of the present lifetime. It is always wise to look to the childhood years when dealing with specific problems, particularly those dealing wtih poor self-images. Children are extremely vulnerable during their early years, since their dominant brain wave patterns are similar to those produced with hypnosis, making them susceptible to programming without the logic and reason functions. Tell a child often enough that he or she is stupid and can't learn, and he or she may have the capacity to be an Einstein but function well below average. Their subconscious has been convinced through repetition. Poor self-images are often the result of thoughtless things said to children: you're clumsy, slow, lazy, ugly, fat, skinny, stupid, can't do anything right, will never be a man, won't ever amount to anything, weak, hysterical, bad, etc. They receive similar programming from commercials. Instead of the emphasis being on building the desirable type of character and personality, they are told that if they wear certain brands of clothing and use certain brands of various products they will be successful and loved, and all will be right in their world. Is it any wonder that there are so many frustrated and unhappy young people in the world when they have been subconsciously programmed to expect so much from superficial things?

To use the regression technique for age regression, simply direct the individual back in this lifetime using birthdays as reference points, and having them scan the time periods between birthdays for significant material. Usually the years prior to age fourteen will contain the most significant material with particular emphasis on the years from zero to six.

If situations are found in which negative programming occurred, you can state at that time: "This statement was mistakenly accepted as fact. It is not true, and you no longer need to react to it." Then, make certain to end the session with the positive statements at the end of the technique.

"Old Home Week"

Several years ago a businessman called and asked for an appointment to be regressed. I have no idea where he got my name. I had never met him before that day, nor have I seen him since.

The regression was progressing well when something began tugging at my memory. He was describing a lifetime as a young woman living in Holland in a family of women. There were several sisters, a mother, an aunt and a grandmother. The men were either all dead or away somewhere. He was one of the sisters. As he recounted various events, I suddenly realized that I had heard this story before from the viewpoint of one of his sisters. While we were talking after the regression, I took a quick look in my files and located the transcript of a regression I had done on a neighbor lady a couple of years earlier. While he was out of the room, I telephoned her and asked if she could come over right away.

A few minutes later she arrived, and when I introduced her to the man, they were both quite puzzled. I sat and listened to them for about ten minutes while they tried to discover where they had met. They were both certain that they knew each other, but couldn't find a single situation in which they might have seen each other before that day. Finally I handed each one the transcript of the other's regression. The recognition was instantaneous, and I sat back and witnessed the most amazing conversation.

Within seconds they were exchanging bits of family gossip, and laughing over incidents from centuries ago as if they had happened only yesterday. They talked about old friends and relatives, new dresses, family celebrations, and re-lived jokes they had played on each other. They reminded me of my aunts at a family reunion.

They must have talked for an hour or more, completely oblivious to my presence, and to the fact that one was a middle-aged farm lady and the other a big city businessman. For that little while they were just two Dutch sisters who hadn't seen each other in a very long while.

Chapter Six

Endings and the Beginning

Death and After

How often it has been said that behind most of men's fears is the fear of the unknown. How often death has been called "The Great Unknown", but it need not be so. One of the most rewarding aspects of regression is the ability to explore one's death experiences. When the unknown becomes familiar, there is nothing to fear.

It might appear from preceding case histories and regressions that most deaths are violent or traumatic in some way. This is not so. Most of the death experiences I have written about were chosen to illustrate some traumatic event which had precipitated influences reaching into present lifetimes, but these are only a tiny percent of the total death experiences explored. By far, the largest number of death experiences are peaceful and welcomed at the end of the intended life span. This is not intended to imply that all planned life spans are long. Many times, for one purpose or another, the intended life span is relatively short because there may be only a limited amount of beneficial experience available within a certain environment or time period to the person involved. Neither should it be assumed from those statements that the time of death is rigidly fixed or predestined, and that one cannot die until his time has come, and when that time has come he cannot escape it. If this was so, then all our efforts to cure illnesses or prevent accidents or protect ourselves from violence are wasted and pointless effort. Man has free will. It is his rightful heritage. If this were not so, then he would be nothing more than a puppet whose strings are manipulated by some greater power, and his accomplishments would be empty and his mistakes without meaning. Life would have no purpose and we might as well all quit right now.

What is death? Man is an unlimited spirit who dwells in houses of flesh and blood in order to be able to manifest himself and experience a physical world. When the house becomes uninhabitable through disease, accident, or age, or man outgrows the usefulness of the house, then man moves on to other realms of experience and leaves the house vacant. Death is no more than that.

Death and birth are, in fact, synonymous. When you die in the physical world you are born into the non-physical realms. When you are born into the physical world, you die to that non-physical existence. Death and birth are both simply changes in your sphere of activity. Just as the great Unlimited Spirit is immortal, so you who were created from His essence, in His image, are immortal.

In order to explore death experiences during the course of a regression, after the lifetime has been explored to the extent desired, direct the individual to:

*Go to the point in time which is the day **before** your death. It will only take a moment. Tell me as soon as you are there. This is simply an exercise in*

remembering. There is no reason for you to feel fear,
pain, distress or apprehension on any level. (Pause for
response.)

Mentally look out through your eyes and listen
through your ears. Where are you, and what are you
doing?

Approximately what age are you?

What is your state of health?

Looking back on your life, are there any events
which you remember and would like to mention which
were not previously remembered?

How do you feel about your life? Did you accom-
plish what you intended with this lifetime?

(Depending upon the answers, you may want to explore
this more fully.)

Ask whatever additional questions that seem appropriate at the moment, depending on the circumstances
discovered. Then:

Now, without experiencing any pain, distress, fear
or apprehension, pass through the experience of your
death and arrive at the day after your death. It will
only take a moment. Tell me when you are there.
This is simply an exercise in remembering.

Are you aware that you are dead?

How did you die?

How do you feel about being dead?

Most people, though not all, are aware that they are
dead and do not exhibit surprise at the continuation of
consciousness. Occasionally, when death has happened
suddenly or unexpectedly through accident or violence,
the individual may not be aware of the change. The change
in consciousness between life and death is so minimal that
about the only difference is a sense of freedom, of no longer
being limited by a physical body. The person may even
attempt to carry out physical actions or communicate with

individuals in the vicinity and be frustrated and confused at the lack of response. If this situation has occurred in the death experience being investigated, give the instructions:

Move to the point in time when you become aware that you are dead.

Then:

What caused you to become aware that you were dead?

For those who are immediately aware of their deaths, which will be the majority, you will find that the consciousness of the individual often remains around to observe the actions of friends and relatives. It is not unusual at all for an individual to observe his own funeral. There is a somewhat detached feeling, though there may be concern or very minimal distress over excessive grief shown by survivors. However, I cannot remember a single instance in all of the regressions I have witnessed where the individual being regressed has exhibited any distress during the death experience, or afterward at the idea of being dead. As strange as it may seem, the period immediately after death often provides some extremely humorous moments due to the observations and comments of 'the deceased'.

After the individual has passed through the death experience, give the instruction:

Go to a point in time about six weeks after your death. It will only take a moment. Tell me as soon as you are there.

Where are you, and what are you doing?

At this point there will probably be little sensory input. People usually describe a feeling of just 'being'. There are no sensations of heat or cold, no sound, usually no visual sensations. The feeling most often described is one of feeling safe, secure and very contented. This seems to be a period of rest and recuperation from the earth experience. Occasionally there may be a vague awareness of others in a similar state nearby. However, even when there is no consciousness of other awarenesses, no one has ever expressed a feeling of loneliness or being alone.

From this point on, time spans are meaningless, as time as we know it does not exist. Time is a concept created for the convenience of physical man.

At some point the individual will emerge from the rest period to undertake an evaluation of the preceding lifetime, and to look at it in the larger framework of other past lifetimes. This is a period of self-judgement in which the person truly meets self and weighs his actions and motivations behind the actions, and begins to form an idea of what needs to be dealt with in future lifetimes. This is often a profound experience because no illusions are allowed. It is the difference between looking at ourselves in a mirror and seeing the self we want to see and being able to ignore what we don't care to acknowledge, and suddenly looking at an unretouched photograph where every blemish and wrinkle and imperfection is revealed. The person reliving this episode may not care to verbalize the details, but it would be valuable to make a private written record afterward for study. This isn't necessarily a completely unpleasant experience. As you add up the pebbles of each action and motivation and the influences set into motion, you may be pleasantly surprised to find how often the balance comes out on the positive side. To direct an individual to this experience, say:

Now move to the period in which you begin your evaluation of your past lifetime.

The sequence is not always consistent, but often after the self-evaluation, the individual will next find himself engaged in some type of learning experience. This can take the form of a group or individual class type situation, or a scenario which is set up for him to 'live' through to understand a particular truth or concept. (The scenario which I experienced after my suicide described in a prior chapter is an example.) Sometime before or after this period, the blueprint for the next lifetime is begun. The general circumstances for the lifetime are chosen: race, social status, economic conditions, spiritual atmosphere, probable career, type of parents, etc. Specifics are added later. It isn't necessary to explore this aspect at this point. The time for that is later when the blueprint is complete.

Since man has free will, in or out of a physical body, sometimes unwise choices are made in laying out the blueprint. Only in very rare, very extreme circumstances does it appear that any type of guidance or suggestion is made from outside sources. Sometimes remorse or great zeal will cause a soul to undertake circumstances and situations which are unrealistic in their expectations. Sometimes we are like a housewife who plans to repaint and redecorate her house and prepare a gourmet spread for a large party all in one day. There may be a rare individual somewhere who could successfully pull it off, but more than likely the housewife is going to end up exhausted, frustrated and in the middle of a tremendous unfinished mess. People can choose such difficult circumstances for a lifetime and overload themselves so in what they want to accomplish in one lifetime that they end up overwhelmed or in a hopeless muddle, so discouraged and frustrated that they accomplish little. And often no flexibility is planned into the blueprint to allow for the free will of others, and choices they may make which will affect the individual's lifetime.

On the other hand, some may choose life circumstances which provide ease and comfort and little challenge. This type of life can be as stupifying and unfulfilling as the other extreme.

A soul is not locked into a blueprint, even after birth. Unwise choices can be changed and life directions can be altered. Sometimes the understanding of the principles involved make it unnecessary to continue a particular course of action. Knowledge can bring understanding which can change a person's outlook. For instance, a person may come to the understanding that he or she is continually involved in cycles of unhappiness or suffering, unwisely having chosen that as a method of karmic penance for past actions. Realizing that karma is intended to teach rather than punish, and that a more positive and productive apprcach is desirable, a person can mentally reject another such cycle and refuse to make the decisions and initiate the actions which perpetuate the cycles. Then, a person can deliberately choose a positive course of action to satisfy the needs of the situation.

Upon occasion when I have recognized the beginning of such a cycle, or the repeat of a cycle which deals with a lesson I have already learned, mentally affirming: "I do not choose to participate in this cycle. It has no positive benefit for me. I choose to move forward to something else.", is enough to change the sequence of events.

Because each of us is different and is dealing with a wide variety of experience, it is difficult to deal with specifics. The best way to tailor this information to your specific situation is, toward the end of a regression, after exploring the death experience, to direct yourself or the person you are regressing to:

> *Come forward in time now to the point in time when you chose your parents for this present lifetime as* _____ _____ *(present name). It will only take a moment. Tell me as soon as you are there.*
>
> *At what time did you choose these people to be your parents?*

The answers will vary widely. Sometimes the choice is made before the parents have even met each other. Sometimes the choice is not made until the pregnancy is established. It varies from person to person. Sometimes information is obtained which was known only to the parents, and can be verified by them if they are open to this type of information: private conversations, private jokes, a favorite dress, a favorite tie, the circumstances of their first meeting, etc.

Then continue:

Why did you choose these two people to be your parents? What lessons did you hope to learn from the particular environment they could provide?

The person may or may not choose to answer these questions aloud.

At this time, you have access to the blueprint which you created for this particular lifetime. Examine it until you have firmly fixed in your awareness what you wanted to accomplish in this lifetime. You may verbalize the information or not as you choose, but tell me when you have the information fixed in your mind.

When the individual has indicated that he or she has finished scanning this information, say:

You may return to this point of awareness any time you desire additional information.

Then go ahead and terminate the session in the same manner outlined in the standard regression technique.

This information can be valuable insight into your life. You may find that you have already accomplished most of what you intended and are therefore free to establish a new set of goals. Perhaps you will find answers to some underlying frustrations in your life. Maybe you have deviated from your blueprint and the things you wanted to accomplish, and this has caused undefined little naggings in your mind which keep you from being really satisfied with your direction. If this is true, then it is time to ask yourself some questions. Has the deviation taken you in a positive, productive direction? Was the deviation by your own will or was it the result of the actions of others over which you had no control? You may find that others made choices and changes between the time you chose your parents and the time that you were born, or at even later times, which changed the circumstances of your environment so radically that you found it necessary to file a whole new 'flight plan'.

If the direction of your life is beneficial in spite of the deviation, or if it was a matter basically beyond your control, mentally affirm that you are letting go of the original blueprint to follow a course of action which is more appropriate for you at this time. You will find that this mental letting go will get rid of many, if not all, of those semi-subconscious frustrations which make you feel that you are not doing quite what you ought to with your life.

On the other hand, if you find that you have deviated from your blueprint for no good reason, and are not making real and solid progress in your spiritual growth, take a good long look at your blueprint and at your life and see what changes you need to make to bring them more in line with each other. There may be compromises that you have to make if you are well along in this lifetime. It may not be realistic to try to rigidly follow the blueprint. A balanced assessment of the situation will show you that it is not so much a matter of what you do as far as careers or hobbies or such things are concerned, as how you do them. Your attitudes in your approach to life will often make the difference in how much you are in harmony with your blueprint. Cultivate fairness, tolerance and kindness, demand the best of yourself and others. Learn to rehearse success in your mind. Nothing comes into being without first being created in the mind. Few people realize how often they rehearse failure in their minds and thus bring it into being. Get into the habit of imaging yourself succeeding at whatever you set out to do. Hold the image of yourself acting and reacting with the qualities of character you desire. The changes won't happen overnight, but soon you will find that what took a conscious effort has become a natural reaction.

Case History

The following is an example of some of the information which is available during the exploration of one's blueprint.

Q: Come forward in time now to the point at which you chose your parents for this present lifetime as _____ _____ (present name). It will only take a moment. Tell me as soon as you are there.

A: All right. I'm there.

Q: At what time did you choose these people to be your parents? Did they already know each other?

A: No, (laughing) this is great. They always allowed me to believe that they met at church, but I see them meeting at a dance. They were both raised in families where dancing was forbidden, and they never allowed me to dance. It seems, from what I see, that Dad often slipped away to dances and movies. Mom went to only one dance with some girl friends, and that is when she met Dad. They liked each other immediately and made arrangements to meet 'properly' at church. He was 19, she was 17. They dated for about six months before they married. I was born about two years later.

Q: Why did you choose these two people to be your parents? What lessons did you hope to learn from the particular environment they could provide? You may answer these questions aloud or not, as you choose.

A: These two people were physically and mentally healthy from long-lived stock. They had strong characters and could provide an unusual combination of a thorough, fundamentally oriented religious background within an environment which encouraged intellectual curiosity.

Q: Had you known these two people in a past life?

A: Not as far as I can determine.

Q: At this time, you have access to the blueprint which you created for this present lifetime. Examine it until you have firmly fixed in your mind what you wanted to accomplish in this lifetime. You may verbalize the information or not, as you choose. Just tell me when you have the information fixed in your mind.

A: This is amazing. I see the whole picture — how the trends and events so far in my life fit together into a logical pattern to help me towards the goals I established in my blueprint. I've never thought of my life as having an overall plan or pattern before, but it is clear now. I see, or know it, as a whole, but I'll try to separate the parts.

My parents and home environment were necessary to provide a healthy body and mind for a demanding lifetime of fairly long span. I set goals of learning to be open-minded and tolerant, developing a strong self-confidence, and understanding the scope of personal responsibility. Self-discipline had been a problem in some past lives, and I also needed to learn to accept myself and my right to venture into whatever areas of learning and development I desired.

Let's see if I can sort this out. I'll try to take it point by point, even though the areas overlap. Open-mindedness and tolerance: I have been a religious bigot in more than one lifetime, while not really living by what I professed to be true. The bigotry was accompanied by a very rigid, closed mind in most areas of life. While the religious training was important from the viewpoint of having a good foundation of Biblical knowledge and developing a strong sense of right and wrong, the environment which pushed me to explore and question and delve into broad areas of knowledge was essential. As I explored and experimented in various areas, I was drawn into learning about world religions, past and present, and into an understanding of the 'spirit of the law' in balance with the 'letter of the law'. I'm not sure at what point that I realized that there is a Universal Law which governs man and has little to do with organized religion, but gives man an almost unlimited scope of endeavor and accomplishment. I'm not sure I've ever tried to put this into words before, and it's hard to say exactly what I mean.

Q: Just take your time. As long as you understand, that's the important thing.

A: The point is, I guess, that man is a lot freer than he allows himself to be. Man's soul came from God and is on its journey back to God. That's what it's all about. But somewhere along the line men started making up a bunch of rules and restrictions about how to make the journey, and all these different religions came into being which really deny and restrict the mystical, spritual nature of man. This is part of what I had to dig out and understand for myself, and I guess I'm still undergoing the process of acceptance on various levels. I don't feel the need to force my views on others, but sometimes I still have to fight a feeling of intolerance and superiority about it. I see that I still have a lot to learn along this line even though I'm no longer a bigot in the true sense of the word.

Q: How has this helped you toward your other goals?

A: Well, it has helped me to develop self-confidence. I've learned to listen to an inner part of myself which seems to know when something is true. And I've learned to respect my own mental abilities. I don't have any college degrees, but I have proved to myself that I can learn and master anything I set my mind to. I've learned not to let the criticism and derision of others undermine my self-esteem or weaken my courage to stand by my convictions. Sometimes that has been a very painful battle in this lifetime. The choice so often seems to be between hurting those I love the most, or being true to what my inner self says is right. I'm not sure I'll ever be, or even want to be, completely comfortable with that. I'm going to have to think some about that particular point. I see that leads into another part of my blueprint — understanding and accepting the limits of personal responsibility and learning not to feel guilty when I can't make everyone happy or solve their problems for them.

This is a little off that subject, but not entirely. I see in the blueprint that I originally planned to be a doctor in this lifetime. That's interesting. I started in that direction with my education, but when other doors opened I quit and did something entirely different. I took a lot of flack from my family about that and I've always felt a little guilty about it. But I see that being a doctor was not the best choice for growing into my blueprint. Somewhere along the line my subconscious must have realized it wasn't the best route for me to take. It's funny how that has nagged at me all these years. It's a relief to really know that I made the right decision, that it wasn't a 'cop-out' the way everyone thought.

I can see how being a doctor would have reinforced the negative side of the tendency I had to feel responsible for everyone. I would have just sunk deeper and deeper into it. As it was, I allowed others to influence me into a false idea of personal responsibility. I became so deeply involved in seemingly charitable and helpful undertakings that I neglected myself and my wife and children. You know the philosophy — you should never do anything for yourself, it should always be for others. I tried to solve everyone's problems but mine and felt responsible for the actions and decisions of those around me. I felt like it was some failure on my part when others did wrong. I spent so many sleepless nights worrying and hurting and feeling guilty because I couldn't get others to stop doing things which caused their own unhappiness. And, no matter what demands were made on me and my time, I couldn't say no. I felt selfish and guilty when I wanted to. It was a harsh lesson I had to learn. I came close to doing a lot of damage to my health and my marriage before I rebelled and cut myself off from everything for a little while. I did a lot of thinking and studying and gradually came to realize that I am only responsible for me and my actions. If I could help someone learn how to solve their own problems, that was true help. I could only share things which I had learned, but I was not responsible for whether or not others used the information. My first responsibility was to myself — to learn to solve my own problems and give attention to my personal growth. And, I wasn't responsible if living true to the principles and values I believed caused some around me to be unhappy because my beliefs differed from theirs and I didn't 'belong to their church'.

I can see that I've accomplished a lot of what is in my blueprint, even though I didn't know I had one until now. There is a lot more that I need to do in these same areas. And I need to concentrate more attention on self-discipline. There is more in the blue-

print that I need to look at and understand, and I
need to think about what I have seen and where I go
from here, but I'm tired right now. Is it possible for
me to come back to this again later?

Q: Certainly. You can return to this point of awareness
anytime you desire additional information. Just relax
and direct your mind to your blueprint. In a moment
I will count from 1 to 5 . . . .

I am often asked if there is a certain period of time
which must pass between lifetimes. There appears to be no
standard length of time between incarnations. Sometimes
centuries elapse between lifetimes, sometimes only months. I
believe that there are many factors involved. Sometimes a
soul must wait for just the right set of circumstances to
occur or a particular world situation. If the person died
prematurely leaving things undone that were very important to him, the time between incarnations is likely to be
short. If the prior lifetime was particularly difficult or
unpleasant, or left some traumatic scar on the soul, then
the soul may be reluctant to reincarnate. Some of these,
I believe, account for some of the stillbirths and newborn
deaths which occur for no discernible physical reason. The
soul panics and backs out.

In other situations, war for instance, where death
occurs in the defense of country or an ideal which is very
important to the person, the soul may return rather quickly
in an effort to continue in that situation. Others may return
quickly in an effort to stop such occurrences. Some of the
very young protesters of the late '60's and '70's whom I
regressed were casualties of World War II and Korea. Others
of that time had come back eager to return to the military.
A couple of the more militant of the anti-nuclear protesters
were casualties of Hiroshima and Nagasaki. There are many
such patterns to be observed. While one might not agree with

a particular movement or philosophy, or the manner in which it is carried out, such knowledge can make one more tolerant and understanding of the motivations of those involved.

As you see, the exploration of death and what occurs afterward can be as exciting and informative as the investigations of past lives.

The Origin of Man

I cannot answer the question of why the Unlimited Spirit chose to create man. But the choice was made and the deed done, and it is possible for you to remember that first moment when you were given the awareness of "I exist", "I am".

After you have experienced regression enough to be comfortable and proficient with the technique, instead of emerging into a past lifetime:

> *You will return to the point of your origin as an individual awareness, the time when the Unlimited Spirit separated you from Itself and gave you the awareness of your own individual existence. When you arrive at that point, you will listen and hear the instructions which were given to you.*

You may wish to experience this for yourself before you read the remainder of this chapter.

It would appear that we, as souls, were sent out on a field trip through the Universe to explore, discover and understand not only all creation but our own natures. Some completed their assignments and returned to the Source. Others of us forgot why we were here, what we are, and where we came from — and here we remain trying to find our way back.

As unlimited spirits, it would seem that we set out upon our journey through the universe, and many of us became intrigued by the physical creatures we observed. We saw that they experienced sensations — heat, cold, hunger, pain, sex, etc. — which we, not having physical bodies, could only wonder about. Having free will, we found that we could project ourselves into those creatures and experience what they experienced. Some souls were content to experience and move on. Others allowed themselves to become entrapped by the physical sensations, and either could not or would not detach themselves from that physical existence.

At some point in time, the Unlimited Spirit took pity upon his wayward children and created human bodies, male and female, as more appropriate vehicles for the soul, giving opportunity for a broader scope of experience.

It is not unusual for those who remember the moment of their creation to undergo the experience described here in the words of one individual:

> *I stood at the very outer limits of the Universe. I could see the whole of Creation spread out in front of me. I felt so insignificant, so infinitesimal in this vast Creation. I experienced an overwhelming, profound sense of being alone — yet I was not alone. Then I understood that I was part of the Whole. This boundless Creation was part of me, and without the tiny cell which I knew as 'me', it would be incomplete.*

I believe that we all, at one time or another, remember that first moment of profound loneliness, but seldom understand what it is. Those moments when we feel such intense longing and loneliness for something or someone which we can't define are echoes of the instant in which we first experienced our separation from our Creator and became aware of our individuality — a soul longing for its Source.

We experience this longing consciously or unconsciously to varying degrees throughout our many lifetimes.

The degree to which we feel separate from our Source is determined by the degree to which we are out of touch with our inner being, which is a part of that Source. I believe that our actions in the physical world are mirrors of the degree of separation we feel. There are individuals who frantically pursue fulfillment in a variety of ways but never seem to find it. They drive themselves in the business world seeking a success which never seems to satisfy a nagging inner hunger. Others attach themselves to one person after another, expecting to find the perfect relationship which will make them feel complete, but are always disappointed and usually blame the other person for not being the right one. Lives are filled with people, noise, activities, alcohol, drugs, casual sex and material acquisitions in an effort to fill the emptiness.

The more frantically and determinedly fulfillment is pursued along these lines, the more a person raises the barriers between himself and that which he is seeking. When the mind is constantly occupied, an individual lacks the opportunity to learn how to be at peace with himself and his thoughts and open the paths of the mind to make contact with his real self, which is a part of the Source.

Past life regression not only has the potential for allowing an individual to recall the experiences of past lifetimes and thereby know himself better and develop a more balanced perspective of life, but it opens access to those deeper levels of mind where communication takes place with our spiritual selves and helps to develop the habit of introspection on those levels. It is through this access that we can understand who and what we are and recover that awareness of being a part of the Whole. That pathway brings a deep sense of contentment and fulfillment.

Chapter Seven

Opening Two Doors

Past life regression is a valuable tool for therapy, whether you are the individual seeking to help yourself, or the professional who is in the business of helping others. It is not necessary for a person to believe in the theory of reincarnation for the regression experience to be a valid and valuable therapy.

Given the opportunity, the mind will seek solutions to problems. If you choose to believe that remembered past lives are but exercises of a vivid imagination, at least those regression experiences do give the individual insight into relationships, causes (whether real or imagined) of problems, traumas, fears and phobias which can be used to alleviate those problems.

The regression experience enhances social counsciousness, generates tolerance and understanding of other cultures, races and the opposite sex, and aids an individual in becoming a better balanced, more complete person. It opens the door to the understanding and shouldering of personal responsibility, and aids individuals in ridding themselves of unnecessary and unhealthy guilt feelings. Personal relationships benefit and a deep, fulfilling insight into one's own nature can be gained.

The regression experience allows individuals to delve into the potentials of their own minds and grasp information, values and understanding on both practical and spiritual levels.

As a therapeutic technique it is not so different from the role-playing techniques which are often used to precipitate a person's understanding of themselves and others. In the case of regression, however, the person chooses for him or herself the role or situation to remember which best meets the needs of the moment. Since this occurs at the deeper Alpha levels of mind, the reliving and release of guilt, fear and negative feelings, and the enhancement of positive feelings and traits have a very real and immediate effect.

Another important aspect of this type of regression therapy is that the individual involved is immediately in the position of taking responsibility for him or herself rather than developing a dependency on the therapist.

The regression experience allows an individual a healthy avenue for the release of anger, frustration and stress, all of which contribute to mental, spiritual and physical dis-ease. With the changes in attitude and life perspective which are usually generated by the regression experience, the individual often finds that there are fewer situations in the future which initiate anger and frustration and cause stress. An individual becomes more relaxed in his or her approach to life and therefore has a healthier mental and emotional state which promotes a healthier body.

Past life and age regression are important tools for therapy with or without the acceptance of reincarnation. When answers to problems cannot be found in the present life, or information uncovered does not appear to hold the complete answer, the use of past life regression opens a door to infinite possibilities for finding solid and beneficial information.

A number of psychiatrists, psychologists and therapists using conventional hypnosis for age regression in search of the causative factors of problems have found themselves in the odd situation of directing a patient to "return to the source of your problem", and having that patient regress to a past life when neither had ever considered the possibility of reincarnation.

Those who continue to discount the possibility of reincarnation after such an experience sometimes offer the explanation that if a situation in the present lifetime is particularly painful, distressing or embarrassing, it may be easier for an individual to begin with it by detaching him or herself from it to a degree in the guise of a past life.

Whatever explanation one chooses to use, the past life regression experience does often engender the courage to understand and deal with problems which might otherwise be avoided. If it brings about positive results with a happier, healthier and more productive individual as the end result, then it seems a tragic waste not to use past life regression as a therapeutic tool whatever the belief about reincarnation.

There are many areas in which little or no work has been done to explore the practical applications of past life regression. The future holds exciting possibilities for those with enough foresight and courage to undertake such research.

Considering the positive results which have been obtained by using past life regression to explore and understand the underlying causes of drug and alcohol addiction in some individuals, I believe that past life regression has the potential for being a valuable tool in understanding what factors contribute to a potentially addictive makeup.

Though little work has been done in this area, a significant enough percent of addicted individuals have found permanent relief through regression to make it a worthwhile avenue to investigate.

I believe that it is not enough that an individual develops the self-control to avoid the use of drugs and alcohol when they are disruptive factors in his or her life. A person has the right of access to methods which will find and eliminate the psychological factors which cause the craving. Such help should not be denied to anyone on the basis of philosophical differences or religious or scientific prejudices.

The use of past life regression offers an open door to the possibility of understanding and eliminating the causes of many of the ills which plague our society. For instance, if a substantial foundation of information could be amassed regarding underlying past life factors which cause some individuals to commit acts of violence, while others from the same background in the present lifetime thrust into the same situations do not, there is a strong probability that potentially violent individuals could be recognized early in life and 'defused' through past life regression. Past life factors, however, must never be allowed to become an excuse for avoiding responsibility for such actions. We are each responsible for our actions and must accept the consequences of those actions. Prevention is the answer.

Since the psychological makeup of an individual often plays a significant role in illness and accidents, it would seem that there is a place here also for the use of past life regression. Certainly the possible past life influences involved in attitudes toward food which cause underweight and overweight problems are worth investigation. There have also been some cases where the origins of allergies have been traced to past life situations.

The scope of the possible applications of past life regression information is only as limited as one's imagination. This is not to suggest that all of the answers to all of the world's problems can be solved through past life regression. There are many answers to be found through the use of this technique, however, in a world in which answers to problems are often all too few.

Perhaps the time will come when past life regression is as much of a rite of passage into adulthood as puberty. Many potential problems could be eliminated before they become handicaps, and positive attitudes and traits could be reinforced.

Regression to Change a World

Those who challenge the theory of reincarnation often attack the premise that all souls were created simultaneously. They argue that if this is so, why has the world population fluctuated so drastically at times, and why is the present world population greater than at any previously known period. Part of the answer lies in the fact that not all souls incarnate at the same time. When a particular world situation offers a broad scope of opportunity for experience and a great potential for spiritual development, more souls incarnate than at times when opportunities are more limited.

Souls who are not incarnated are not dormant. They have periods of learning and growth in non-physical planes of existence where time as we measure it in the physical world does not exist. While they are learning on those planes, they are also watching and waiting for the optimum conditions for further experience in the physical plane to occur.

It must be also taken into account that estimates of the world populations in the past are not necessarily accurate, and do not take into consideration any evidence which may support the probable existence of highly technological societies which have destroyed themselves in the distant past. Even if one discounts the stories of Lemuria,

Atlantis, and an ancient civilization on the site of the present Gobi Desert, one must take into consideration the fact that modern man is not always as knowledgeable about things as he supposes himself to be.

We were all raised with the "historical fact" that Columbus discovered America in 1492. Remember having to memorize that 'fact' for your history tests? Now we are learning that Columbus was a latecomer. It even appears that the Vikings were far down the list of visitors to the 'New World'. There is mounting evidence, gathered by reputable scholars, that North America was a crossroads of international travel and trade hundreds, perhaps thousands of years before 1492. There is strong archeological evidence that 'modern man' may have developed here and then migrated to other parts of the planet rather than the reverse.

Not so many years ago an atom was defined as the smallest, indivisable particle of matter. Almost any school child now knows about protons, neutrons, and electrons and a myriad of other facts about the structure of an atom.

When the automobile was invented there were learned men who were convinced that the human body would disintegrate at 60 m.p.h. Well, under certain circumstances it does, but not from the causes they assumed. Man has reached speeds which were considered fantasy a hundred years ago, and has even stepped into space. But for all that man has learned and accomplished, he is still wondering about his origin. Did he evolve, or was he created? Or was it a combination of the two? Was the universe created, or did it happen with a big bang? Is it expanding or shrinking? Is our planet headed toward an ice age, or is it getting hotter? Why did the dinosaur disappear? You can hear a hundred theories put forward as fact.

The point is that what we believe as fact today probably will have changed by tomorrow as we continue to learn about our world. Even the facts we think we know about yesterday or thousands or millions of years ago are open to interpretation and change. Who really knows what civilizations may have existed in the past to have vanished without a trace?

The significant fact from all of this is that there *are* more souls incarnated at the present time than during any recent historical period, indicating that the opportunities offered for growth and accomplishment are broad and significant. Because of the strength of our numbers, we have the potential for making vast, far-reaching changes in our world. We may make terrible mistakes which could destroy our present environment and negate all of our technological advances. We could become one of those 'lost civilizations' whose very existence is considered pure fable sometime in the distant future. Or, we can make the decision to use our collective potential to remember and understand past errors in judgement and action, and refuse to repeat the destructive cycles.

We are each personally responsible for the role which we play in the destiny of our civilization. We must be willing to take the time and make the effort to understand our past lives, not just as they relate to our present individual selves, but how our actions, inactions and attitudes contributed to the rise or fall of the civilizations we lived in.

After the initial experiences of exploring past lives and coming to a better understanding of ourselves, then we need to take a long, hard look at the social consicousness we exhibited in past lives and ask ourselves some questions.

Were there lifetimes in which we saw injustices taking place around us, and we went along with the crowd because that was the easiest and safest thing to do? Or, did we militantly wade in and flail away without thinking through a responsible course of action, and only succeed in generating conflict? Was it easy to convince ourselves to sit back and do nothing because we told ourselves that one voice wouldn't count for much, and what could one person do? Perhaps it took some personal injustice to stir us to action. Was care and concern for others the motivating force, or was it a desire for personal revenge?

Were there lifetimes when we arrogantly attributed to ourselves a godlike wisdom, and set ourselves above others saying that 'the masses' did not have the intellectual capacity to decide the everyday aspects of life for themselves, that in our superiority we must tell them how to dress, what to eat, what to think, how to raise their children, how to worship God, and even what god to worship? Did we tell them and ourselves that for their own good we must limit their personal freedoms and their scope of choice? Did we do that, or were we among those who allowed it to be done to us?

Did we arbitrarily declare that any political belief which differed from ours was wrong, any religious belief which differed from ours in error, and any social or cultural practice which differed from ours inferior? Did we feel that those differences gave us the right to apply force, oppression or even death to bring them into line with what was 'right'? Did we try to force our beliefs on those around us in a militant and dogmatic way, thereby blocking the possibility that peaceful discussion might bring about increased knowledge, understanding and tolerance on both sides?

Were there lifetimes in which we allowed ourselves to be lazy and indifferent as personal freedoms slipped away, one by one? Each change seemed small and didn't have much effect on our personal lives at the time. Perhaps it bothered us a little, but we pacified ourselves by thinking that someone else would speak up and do something — and then one day it was too late.

Were there times when we wanted to stand up and defend principles which we knew were just and right, but we were afraid? Did each of us at some time have the capacity to be the one voice of reason in the land that might have stirred others to speak up and take action to change things? Did we remain silent? When voices of reason were raised in the land and warned of the course of the future, did we listen and take action, or did we tell ourselves, "It can't happen here."? When slaughters of vast numbers of people were taking place, did we ignore it and excuse ourselves by trying to believe that it couldn't possibly be true? There are the souls of six million Jews to testify that such things can and do happen. An estimated *nineteen million* Indians in North, South, and Central America and Mexico were slaughtered during the 16th Century in the name of conquest and Christianity. These are only two examples of such things which have happened, and are happening today.

When challenged to take arms in a battle worth fighting, did you plunge in and give it your best, or did you sit back and piously quote, "The meek shall inherit the earth," to justify noninvolvement, not knowing that the word meek originated from a very select group of men who were trained, armed, carefully prepared and alert to act as a defensive force in any situation which might arise?

If you have any knowledge at all of history, then you know that great civilization and empires have risen and fallen. Where are the great Roman, Persian, and Ottoman Empires, or the Aztecs and Mayans, to name a few? It is the nature of such political and cultural structures that they rise to greatness, and then when they seem the most invincible, internal decay begins either a swift or subtle decline. If you believe in reincarnation and take the time to consider your past lives on a broad scale, then you must inevitably find that somewhere, sometime, you played varying roles in the building and destruction of nations. It will also become evident that neither one man nor one small group of men ever really chart the course of history.

It is what the great numbers of ordinary citizens allow a few to do which writes the pages of history.

As you examine the social structures of the time and places where you have lived past lifetimes and remember the attitudes you exhibited and the roles you played, look at the world around you now and compare those memories with your attitudes and roles today. Ask yourself the same questions about today which you have asked yourself about the many yesterdays. Allow what is good, strong and constructive to be fully integrated into your present self. Weed out those attitudes which were destructive and caused conflict, but remember them so that you do not make the same errors again. The world which we shape by our present action or inaction is the world which not only will our children and grandchildren inherit, but we, too, in our future lifetimes.

The law of cause and effect has a collective application in that the progress and benefits we all enjoy today are the effects of things set into motion in other lifetimes. Just as truly, the problems and negative situations that we, the human race, have to deal with are the collective effects of our past actions.

As we learn from the past, — and how often has it been said that the tragedy of the human race is that it never learns from the past — we must accept our personal responsibility to demand responsible actions from those who lead our nations and shape our technology. We can look and see that it has been and is human nature to rush headlong to embrace anything which is presented in the name of progress or technological advancement. We must learn from the past and be more selective about what we are willing to accept.

As an example, if there are side effects or damage to the planet or waste products created, we must demand that our scientists and technicians find a responsible way to deal constructively with those *before* the discovery is implemented. If such a responsible course of action had been demanded in the past, we would not have the present problems of chemical waste pollution and the safe disposal of nuclear waste. We wouldn't be worrying about what additives in our highly processed foods are doing to our bodies, or buying books, tapes and joining clubs in the pursuit of physical fitness because we have so many labor-saving devices that they are killing us through lack of exercise.

We must be willing to ask ourselves if the advantages of a discovery truly outweigh the long range disadvantages, and whether it is progress or another way of repeating a destructive cycle from the past.

Responsible progress and technological advancement is a boon to all mankind. Irresponsible progress and technological advancement generates one destructive side effect after another.

The same is true of responsible and irresponsible help, be it the immediate relief of a starving man or nation, or social or welfare programs. As you look at the past and the present, you will see that mankind has a habit of rallying to the immediate needs of a situation, but rarely attacks the cause of the problem, and usually gives help which creates a dependency on that help. There is an often quoted Chinese proverb which says, "Give a man a fish and you feed him for a day. Teach a man to fish and you feed him for a lifetime." But even that does not go far enough. We must learn and teach others to 'fish' responsibly and take care that there will be an abundance of fish for our lifetimes and future generations.

True help of a material nature should meet the present need, but the major part of that help should be in equipping an individual with the tools or knowledge to help himself solve or avoid the situation which brought about the need to begin with. The past is full of examples which teach us that if we allow ourselves to fall into the trap of solving another's problems, those problems or similar ones tend to recur, and the person still doesn't know what to do. If, however, we see that a person is equipped with whatever he needs to solve his own problem, and the responsibility for solving the problem is left in his hands, then he learns how to deal with that situation for the present and in the future.

The past should teach us several things about helping others: if a person really wants to solve a problem, he will find a way; what we or another might see as the proper help for a situation may not be; and sometimes the best help you can give to another is no help. Help which creates a dependency can have a many faceted result. At first the giver of help may feel a sense of satisfaction and an ego boost, then continued dependency usually results in resentment, anger and rejection. The recipient of the help usually feels an immediate relief, then a sense of helplessness when the situation continues or recurs, then anger at eventual rejection. Often the recipient of unwise help develops the attitude that the world owes him or her unlimited help. The world owes us nothing. We are the debtors.

If enough people use past life regression to know themselves and thereby know and understand their fellow-men, and to understand the mistakes of the past and refuse to repeat them, we have a chance to become a world which is peopled by tolerant, responsible, peaceful human beings. This can become the Age of Man which is characterized by the triumph of having learned from the past. We can turn our thoughts and energies from wondering whether our world will be blighted by a nuclear holocaust or wiped out by famine, and concentrate on the reason for our continued presence in the cycle of reincarnation — remembering who and what we are, and how to return to the Source from which we came.

A Last Word

The tools are yours. Use them as you choose, but use them wisely. Do not be hesitant to explore new realms or to greet the information with a healthy skepticism. Any belief which cannot stand up to questioning and repeated examination should be suspect. But do not discard information just because it is new or different from what you have believed. Test it and work with it until it is proven true or false. Have the courage to challenge yourself and your beliefs, and strive for the truth which brings freedom.

There is something which can be said about regression which can be said about little else in our present world: It is neither immoral, illegal nor fattening, and it doesn't cause cancer in laboratory mice. Your only investment is a relatively small amount of time. So, feel free to indulge often. It is interesting and fun, and the rewards can be enormous.

STAY IN TOUCH

On the following pages you will find listed, with their current prices, some of the books and tapes now available on related subjects. Your book dealer stocks most of these, and will stock new titles in the Llewellyn series as they become available. We urge your patronage.

However, to obtain our full catalog, to keep informed of new titles as they are released and to benefit from informative articles and helpful news, you are invited to write for our bi-monthly news magazine/catalog. A sample copy is free, and it will continue coming to you at no cost as long as you are an active mail customer. Or you may keep it coming for a full year with a donation of just $2.00 in U.S.A. ($7.00 for Canada & Mexico, $10.00 overseas, first class mail). Many bookstores also have *The Llewellyn New Times* available to their customers. Ask for it.

Stay in touch! In *The Llewellyn New Times'* pages you will find news and reviews of new books, tapes and services, announcements of meetings and seminars, articles helpful to our readers, news of authors, advertising of products and services, special money-making opportunities, and much more.

The Llewellyn New Times
P.O. Box 64383-Dept. 510, St. Paul, MN 55164-0383, U.S.A.

• • •

TO ORDER BOOKS AND TAPES

If your book dealer does not have the books and tapes described on the following pages readily available, you may order them direct from the publisher by sending full price in U.S. funds, plus $1.00 for handling and 50¢ each book or item for postage within the United States; outside USA surface mail add $1.00 extra per item. Outside USA air mail add $7.00 per item.

FOR GROUP STUDY AND PURCHASE

Because there is a great deal of interest in group discussion and study of the subject matter of this book, we feel that we should encourage the adoption and use of this particular book by such groups by offering a special "quantity" price to group leaders or "agents".

Our Special Quality Price for a minimum order of five copies of PAST LIFE REGRESSION is $20.85 Cash-With-Order. This price includes postage and handling within the United States. Minnesota residents must add 6% sales tax. For additional quantities, please order in multiples of five. For Canadian and foreign orders, add postage and handling charges as above. Credit Card (VISA, MasterCard, American Express, Diners' Club) Orders are accepted. Charge Card Orders only may be phoned free ($15.00 minimum order) within the U.S.A. by dialing 1-800-THE MOON (in Canada call: 1-800-FOR-SELF). Customer Service calls dial 1-612-291-1970 and ask for "Kae". Mail Orders to:

LLEWELLYN PUBLICATIONS
P.O. Box 64383-Dept. 510 / St. Paul, MN 55164-0383, U.S.A.

THE EYE OF THE CENTAUR
by Barbara Hand Clow

This book tells a wonderful story of personal and spiritual evolution, as it illustrates a new approach to the practice of Past Life Regression as a vehicle for spiritual growth and transformation. Through a direct collaboration with the Higher Self, past lifetimes of high development and the original experience of initiatory energies are brought into the mind and body of the present self. These memories holographically attune the present personality with its own history as a being. Because these past experiences are of one's own being, they are preintegrated with the energy patterns of the present person, they emerge as quickly as the Higher Self will allow, and they show a contextual framework for putting transformation into practice.

In reading *The Eye of the Centaur,* you are looking directly into the way Past Life Regression can connect past and present into a whole greater than its parts; as meanwhile you enter into the inner experience of those skilled in ancient mystery practices of cultures going back through the Celtic, Ancient Greek, Egyptian, and on back into the evolutionary times of Atlantis.

0-87542-095-8, 260 pagaes, 6 x 9, illus., softcover. $9.95

DAYDREAM YOUR WAY TO SUCCESS
by William Hewitt

There is no other hypnosis book on the market that has the depth, scope, and explicit detail as does this book. The exact and complete wording of dozens of hypnosis routines is given. Real case histories and examples are included for a broad spectrum of situations. Precise instructions for achieving self-hypnosis, the alpha state, and theta state are given. There are dozens of hypnotic suggestions given covering virtually any type of situation one might encounter. The book tells how to become a professional hypnotist. It tells how to become expert at self-hypnosis all by yourself without external help. And it even contains a short dissertation going "beyond hypnosis" into the realm of psychic phenomena. There is something of value here for nearly everyone.

This book details exactly how to gain all you want—to enrich your life at every level. No matter how simple or how profound your goals, this book teaches you how to realize them. The book is not magic; it is a powerful key to unlock the magic within each of us.

0-87542-300-0, 180 pages, 5¼ x 8, softcover. $6.95

Past Life Regression Tapes
William Hewitt

Llewellyn offers a set of two tapes on current and Past Life Regression. Please write for our free catalog.

METAPHYSICS: THE SCIENCE OF LIFE
by Anthony J. Fisichella

There are thousands of books and articles on metaphysical" subjects, such as the meaning of life, the nature of God, the teachings of various religions, reincarnation, life after death, the various disciplines such as astrology, numerology, tarot, ESP research, healing, and many others. Is there a golden thread of wisdom" which encompasses a broad-based understanding of the essential truths of the various teachings? Is there a primer where one can learn the fundamental concepts, the common denominator present in most spiritual teachings?

There is now, in Tony Fisichella's **METAPHYSICS: THE SCIENCE OF LIFE.** For the first time, here is one book which ties together the ancient and modern teachings about human life—which answers the basic questions that most thinking people ask: who am I, where did I come from, what am I here for, where am I going? Here is a book which can change your way of thinking, which can provide the reference you need to help solve practical problems, to find the direction you seek, to understand the teachings of great relgions in their true context. Here is a book which can truly change your life.

ISBN: 0-87542-229-2 $9.95

THE ART OF SPIRITUAL HEALING
by Keith Sherwood

Each of you has the potential to be a healer; to heal yourself and to become a channel for healing others. Healing energy is always flowing through you. Learn how to recognize and tap this incredible energy source. You do not need to be a victim of disease or poor health. Rid yourself of negativity and become a channel for positive healing.

Become acquainted with your three auras and learn how to recognize problems and heal them on a higher level before they become manifested in the physical body as disease.

Special techniques make this book a "breakthrough" to healing power, but you are also given a concise, easy-to-follow regimen of good health to follow in order to maintain a superior state of being.

ISBN: 0-87542-720-0, soft cover, illsutrated. $7.95